# Advance Praise for
## *Inspiration to Perspiration*

"If you're ready to achieve your goals, read this inspiring book. Let *Inspiration to Perspiration* serve as your road map to success."

—Ken Blanchard, co-author of
*The One Minute Manager®*

"The people and knowledge contained here will help you accomplish your meaningful goals. Take your inspiration and move ahead today to a little perspiration."

—Bernie Siegel, M.D., author of
*Love, Medicine & Miracles* and
*Prescriptions for Living*

"Success must be earned, BUT the path to success can be learned. *Inspiration to Perspiration* will help you reach your goals faster, more directly, and more enjoyably."

—Marty Liquori,
NBC Olympic commentator and
Team In Training National Chairman

"*Inspiration to Perspiration* will show you how to turn an idea or a glimmer of hope into reality. The sections on inspiration and networking are critical and often ignored components of effective goal setting. I was moved to tears and inspired by many of the individual stories of people who stretched themselves to achieve challenging goals they never before thought possible."

—Patricia Zigarmi, co-author of
*Leadership and the One Minute Manager®* and
Consulting Partner, The Ken Blanchard Companies

"The stories in this book show you just how powerful goals can be as motivators for achievement. Even more importantly, *Inspiration to Perspiration* shows you how to set and reach your own significant goals."

—David Berke, Senior Program Associate,
Center for Creative Leadership

# INSPIRATION

## TO

# PERSPIRATION

# INSPIRATION
## TO
# PERSPIRATION

The **4** Essential Steps to
Achieving Your Goals

DAVID A. JACOBSON

GOAL SUCCESS, Inc.

Published by Goal Success, Inc.
10601 Tierrasanta Blvd., Suite 402
San Diego, CA 92124
Phone: (858)715-1784  Fax: (858)715-1616

Blood cancer facts on pages 52 through 55 excerpted with permission from The Leukemia & Lymphoma Society's "Facts 2002."

Thanks also go to the individuals profiled throughout the book for allowing us to share their amazing stories.

Publisher's Cataloging-in-Publication Data
Jacobson, David A.
    Inspiration to perspiration: the four essential steps to achieving your goals / David A. Jacobson. -- San Diego, CA : Goal Success, 2003.

    p. ; cm.

    ISBN 0-9728426-0-8

    BF637.S4 J33 2003          2003102120
    158.1-dc21                 0305

Cover design by Kelli Leader
Interior design by Debbie Sidman/Paw Print Media

PROJECT COORDINATION BY JENKINS GROUP, INC. WWW.BOOKPUBLISHING.COM

Printed in the United States of America

07  06  05  04  03  •  5  4  3  2  1

*This book is dedicated to my wife Shari
and my son Sean, my true
and everlasting inspirations.*

# Contents

## Part One: Develop Winning GAIN Plans  11
### The Four Essential Steps to Achieving Your Goals

## Part Two: Inspiration and Perspiration  77
### Inspiring True Stories from Team In Training

# Part Three: Your Success Toolbox          139
### *Step-by-Step Guidance for Developing Your Own Winning GAIN Plans*

# Acknowledgments

W riting this book has mirrored the process it describes. *Inspiration to Perspiration* has been over three years in the making and would not have been possible without the dedication and support of many people. Special thanks go to the following:

To my wife Shari and my son Sean for their support and understanding through this entire process. Your love and encouragement inspire me every day. Also, a special thank you to Shari for all of your help coordinating this project, reviewing each manuscript draft, and giving me the honest feedback I know I can count on from you.

To my parents, Rosie and Bob Jacobson, for teaching me at an early age that I could accomplish anything I set my mind to. I love you.

To my sister Julie, my brother Michael, and my sister-in-law Melanie for your continued encouragement and support.

To my mother-in-law and father-in-law, Zita and Morris Liebermensch, for your unwavering support and encouragement. You are a blessing in my life.

To Matt Treger, my lifelong friend and business partner, who helped me get the book across the finish line.

To the story contributors who opened their hearts and their lives to inspire readers. I consider each of you a friend and thank you for sharing your lessons in courage, hope, and perseverance.

To all of my friends and colleagues at The Leukemia & Lymphoma Society. Without your support and collaboration this book would not have been possible. Your dedication to your cause is unmatched. Special thanks to Cynthia Cross, Greg Elfers, Ellen Curtis, Keith Turner, Peter West, Dwayne Howell, Robin Kornhaber, Dr. Marshall Lichtman, Jeanine Smith, Rick Geswell, Marty Siederer, and Vicki Weiland.

To my friends and associates who read early drafts of the manuscript and offered comments on how to improve the book: Angie and Devin Fitzmaurice, Melanie and Michael Jacobson, Zita Liebermensch, David Berke, Pat Zigarmi, Jimmie Brockbank, and Jennifer and Howard Weitzner.

To Rod Thorn, my editor, who helped me shape and polish the manuscript and who made the stories live up to their potential.

To the entire team at the Jenkins Group, who made my vision of this book a reality.

# Inspiration to Perspiration Online

As you read *Inspiration to Perspiration* you will discover that you are learning essential strategies for success, meeting truly inspiring people, and acquiring powerful tools for achieving your goals. To get the most out of your experience and to ensure that your journey continues after the final chapter of the book, make sure to visit *Inspiration to Perspiration* online at *www.goalsuccess.com*. There you will find an online resource packed with information, inspiration, and tools to help you pursue your goals.

Here is just some of what you will find:

- Online goal planning tools
- PDF files of all the forms in the book
- Additional inspiring true stories
- Updates, photos, poetry, original music compositions, and other content related to the amazing people featured throughout *Inspiration to Perspiration.*

We look forward to seeing you online.

# Foreword

E very once in a while, a book comes along that can help you transform dreams into reality. *Inspiration to Perspiration* is that kind of
book. Author David Jacobson draws on his experience as a corporate leadership trainer, team builder, executive coach, and endurance athlete to
give you a simple yet powerful process for getting more of what you want
out of life. David has packed this book full of information, tips, and tools
to help you set goals and create action plans to reach them.

This book's mission—*to help you turn your wishes, hopes, and dreams
into reality*—has inspired some truly courageous people to tell you their
stories. These uplifting tales from cancer survivors, their family members,
and the athletes who train and compete to raise money to cure blood
cancers should help inspire you to fulfill your own potential. And since
some of the proceeds from the sale of this book will benefit The Leukemia
& Lymphoma Society's cause, you are also contributing to a brighter
future for others.

You are at the starting line of an exciting journey—the journey to
reach your life's goals. At the Society, we are on a journey as well. Our goal
is to find cures for blood cancers—leukemia, Hodgkin and non-Hodgkin
lymphoma and myeloma—that affect more than 616,000 Americans. We
do this by raising funds for cancer research and patient support services.
While the Society has a number of successful fundraising programs, Team
In Training® (TNT) is by far our most successful. Each year, TNT trains
more than 30,000 aspiring athletes of all fitness levels to complete
endurance events—marathons, half marathons, triathlons, and 100-mile
(century) cycling events—in exchange for raising money to help find cures
for blood cancers. David has highlighted TNT throughout this book as an
example of how the concepts discussed here work when put into action.
And they do work.

Team In Training is the world's largest and most successful combination
endurance sports training and fundraising program. Since its inception in
1988, as a program initiated by Society volunteer Bruce Cleland in New

York, TNT has raised more than $385 million. In the process, it has helped more than 150,000 people just like you reach their fitness goals.

By combining the concepts and tools he uses with corporate executives and teams, with examples from Team In Training, David offers a sure-fire formula for realizing your dreams. I hope you will enjoy the journey on which *Inspiration to Perspiration* leads you. Good luck as you work towards reaching your important life goals.

*Dwayne Howell*
*President and CEO,*
*The Leukemia & Lymphoma Society*

# Introduction

In December of 1997 I opened the mail to find a purple and green post card from The Leukemia & Lymphoma Society's Team In Training program. I saw the words, "We will train you to run a marathon . . ." and quickly threw the card in the trash. As a recreational runner, I thought marathons were for elite athletes, not for ordinary people like me.

At the time I was a trainer for the Center for Creative Leadership, a leadership education organization. I was doing what I loved: leadership training, team building, executive coaching, and organizational development. While the programs I led were about professional growth, often I'd talk with participants about issues of family, life balance, the difficulties of communication, and their goals. When you get right down to it, my work then and now is focused on helping people reach their challenging goals. Even so, the goal of running a marathon was one I'd never considered.

The bright-colored postcard caught my wife Shari's eye when she was emptying the garbage. Fishing it out, she read it more thoroughly than I had. It explained that Team In Training trains individuals of **all fitness levels** to complete a variety of endurance races. In exchange, participants raise funds for blood cancer research and patient support services.

Shari suggested we attend an informational meeting. She was curious to know how Team In Training proposed to train her—a self-proclaimed non-athlete and couch potato—to run a marathon.

A few weeks later we crowded into the lobby of our local blood bank (no coincidence, I'm sure, that the meeting was held there) with 75 other curious people. As we looked around the room, we noticed poster-size pictures of blood cancer patients. Some were survivors, others were still undergoing treatment, and still others had succumbed to their diseases. Many of the posters pictured children. It was our first introduction to the thousands of people afflicted with blood cancers. Little did we know how much their stories would come to impact our lives.

As we waited together for the evening's program, we had no idea that we were standing at the starting line of a life-changing experience.

*Five months later . . .*

As I lay on my back in bed, my legs cramping and my entire body cursing me for what I'd put it through the day before, I thought about going back to sleep. I'd reschedule my meetings. There's always tomorrow, I reasoned.

Shari and I had done it. We'd completed the 26.2 miles and raised a combined $4,500 for charity. We could move on now, right? Satisfied, I closed my eyes and settled back in. But there were nagging questions. How had we done it? Why was the Team In Training program consistently so successful? How could it be used as a metaphor for creating success in other areas of life?

Instinctively, I felt for the hospital bracelet I still had around my wrist. It had been my constant companion and my inspiration from that first meeting in the blood bank all the way through the race. I raised my arm and absent-mindedly looked at the bracelet. I slowly twisted it so I could see the inscription on the other side. It read, "Laura Williams, age 5, ALL." Laura was my honored patient. I'd been matched with her when I joined the program and had run the marathon in her honor. The abbreviation, ALL, stood for acute lymphocytic leukemia, the most common form of childhood leukemia. Laura was bravely battling this disease.

I remembered how Laura, and the bracelet, and the cheering throngs of Team In Training supporters lining the marathon route had willed Shari and me and the thousands of other runners to keep going. How they served as our inspiration as we labored to finish the marathon. I remembered how their energy carried my feet, step by step, and how I had vowed, somewhere about the eighteenth mile, that I would write this book.

You see, I knew there was a connection between Team In Training's ability to help its participants reach their fitness and fundraising goals and my ability to help the individuals and teams I work with reach their personal and professional goals.

I committed myself to finding that connection and writing a book that would reach far more people than either Team In Training or my work could alone. I did briefly consider that it might have been the "endorphins talking" during the race, or that I might have been experiencing a "runner's high."

But I knew differently. There was more to it than the fact that I'd finished a marathon. In my heart I knew I had to take the next step, for Laura, for others like her, and for anyone else who has the courage to dream of a brighter future.

So I turned the bracelet back around, lowered my arm, and pushed myself out of bed, gingerly. I was about to start a new marathon—the integration of what works for my clients with insights from Team In Training's extraordinary success. The book you are holding is the result of that effort. I hope it has the same impact on your life that the postcard had on mine.

*David A. Jacobson*

# The Starting Line

D o you know what you want out of life? Are you willing to take the steps necessary to get it? Are you ready to turn your wishes, hopes, and dreams into reality?

If so, then this book has the information, inspiration, and tools you will need to begin reaching your most important goals today.

In *Inspiration to Perspiration* you will find:

- A proven process for achieving your goals called GAIN Planning™
- Examples of effective GAIN Planning in action, in The Leukemia & Lymphoma Society's Team In Training program
- True stories of courage, hope, and perseverance to inspire you to work towards your significant goals
- A toolbox overflowing with resources to help you set goals and create solid action plans to reach them

In short, you will find a road map to success.

## Part One: Develop Winning GAIN Plans

### The Four Essential Steps to Achieving Your Goals

The heart of *Inspiration to Perspiration* is a simple yet powerful process for achieving goals called GAIN Planning. It is named for the acronym GAIN, which represents the four essential steps you must take to reach your goals:

# GAIN Planning

**STEP 1** **G** oal: Set Specific and Challenging Goals

**STEP 2** **A** ction: Create Detailed and Realistic Action Plans

**STEP 3** **I** nspiration: Identify Compelling Inspirations

**STEP 4** **N** etwork of Support: Build Strong Networks of Support

Combining specific and challenging goals with detailed and realistic action plans, compelling inspirations, and strong networks of support sets you up for success every time. This is the power of GAIN Planning and why Team In Training is so successful.

Whatever your goal, going back to school, getting into better shape, learning a new skill, changing careers, or anything else, creating a GAIN Plan is an important key to your success.

Developing GAIN Plans for each of your goals helps you identify where you are, where you want to go, and how you plan to get there. It helps you crystallize your inspiration, which sustains you along the way. And, it encourages you to enlist the help you will need from others to reach your goals.

*Inspiration to Perspiration* will teach and inspire you to create powerful GAIN Plans for achieving all of your goals.

# GAIN Planning in Action

## *The Team In Training Program*

During my five-month participation in Team In Training, I was amazed as I watched a group of ordinary people transform themselves into marathon runners.

How were these people, some of whom could not run even one mile at the start of the program, able to reach the level of peak performance required to complete a 26.2-mile marathon? Even more intriguing, how are over 30,000 people every year consistently accomplishing similar feats? The answer is that Team In Training is unmatched in its ability to help its participants accomplish each of the four steps in the GAIN Planning process.

The Team In Training program will serve as an example, throughout this book, of the successful results of GAIN Planning. As you learn about each of the critical steps to reaching a goal, you will see how Team In Training enables its participants to take that step.

Team In Training is an awesome example of the individual and collective accomplishments that can result when you combine all the elements of a successful GAIN Plan.

# Part Two: Inspiration and Perspiration

## *Inspiring True Stories from Team In Training*

Part Two is a collection of stories shared by Team In Training athletes, cancer patients, and their family members. The courage, commitment, and selflessness of these amazing people will uplift and inspire you to strive for goals you never before dreamed possible.

*Why did the Indiana University School of Medicine award a 14-year-old cancer patient with an honorary doctor of medicine degree?*

*How did a young women cheat her death sentence and go on to run a marathon in her grandmother's honor?*

*What forced a woman to redefine herself from couch potato to athlete?*

*How did the experience of surviving cancer as a teenager, running a half marathon, and carrying the Olympic torch change a young athlete's life forever?*

*What inspired 19 high school students to train for a marathon and raise over $100,000 for charity in the process?*

You will find the answers to these questions and much more in the inspirational stories in Part Two. They are tales of triumph and courage, shared by people who have overcome obstacles, fears, and disappointments to accomplish feats they never before thought possible.

You may choose to read these stories first. That's fine. They don't need to be read in any particular order. You can read them all at once, or just one or two at a time. You may want to read a few whenever you need a dose of inspiration. Some of the stories may touch you in such a way that you are compelled to read them again and again.

As you read these stories, you will see that many are works in progress. These individuals are still working towards their goals, fighting their diseases, and inspiring others with their courage. I know you will be eager to learn more about these people and to follow their progress. You can, by going to *Inspiration to Perspiration* online at *www.goalsuccess.com*. There you will find bonus material including photos, poetry, artwork, original music compositions, story updates, and additional inspiring stories. You can also send messages to the authors of the stories, letting them know how their story impacted you.

# Part Three: Your Success Toolbox

### Step-by-Step Guidance for Developing Your Own Winning GAIN Plans

After learning the GAIN Planning process, hearing about Team In Training, and reading the success stories of people involved in it, I know you will be motivated to start working towards your own goals. Part Three, *Your Success Toolbox,* has all the tools you will need to create winning GAIN Plans for your goals.

In Part Three you'll find:

1. Step-by-step guidance for creating individual GAIN Plans
2. Step-by-step instructions for facilitating a team goal setting session and for creating team GAIN Plans
3. A section for teens and the people who care about their success, with guidance on selecting the right goals and asking for help from the right people
4. Over 20 different downloadable GAIN Planning forms with instructions on how to put them to use
5. Information about creating GAIN Plans online
6. Additional resources to assist you in reaching your goals

As you cross the starting line of this book, you are beginning a journey towards making your dreams reality. You may choose to walk your path, reading a little bit at a time while working to integrate the concepts into your life as you go. Or, you may choose to sprint towards the end, reading the entire book all at once. Either way, your journey will not always be smooth. The concepts presented here are straightforward and easy to understand, but putting them into action requires commitment and determination. I know you can do it! I encourage you to exert the sweat and effort necessary to see the journey through. Doing so has the ability to make a powerful difference in your life!

Let's begin!

# Team In Training
*By Janice "Jo" Stahl*

Life is a journey, a marathon.
It begins.
It ends.
Life is a contest of endurance with hills and valleys,
peaks and depths.
A roller coaster ride.
One we have little say in the choosing.
Captives of the rail, we journey from beginning to end.
Along the way, we learn that what is important is not
the speed with which we traverse the distance, but the determination
with which we traverse it.
There will be those who begin with swiftness and sureness only to
finish laboriously and with uncertainty.
Others will begin slowly and gain momentum
to rage towards the finish line.
But, no matter.
We will all reach the finish line.
There will be no losers.
Each of us benefiting from the richness of the journey.
Sometimes, benefiting from the journey of others.

# PART ONE

## Develop Winning GAIN Plans

*The Four Essential Steps
to Achieving Your Goals*

*You are never given a wish without also being given the power
to make it come true. You may have to work for it, however.*

Richard Bach

# Set Specific and Challenging Goals

*If one does not know to which port one is sailing,*
*no wind is favorable.*

Seneca

Reaching a long sought-after goal is one of the most fulfilling aspects of being alive. Whether it's climbing a mountain, graduating from high school, completing a marathon, getting married, landing a great job, or winning an Oscar, reaching significant goals makes life exciting.

The goals we set guide our decisions, impact our happiness, and serve as the measuring sticks by which we judge our success.

In my work developing individual leaders and teams and in my interviews with Team In Training athletes and cancer patients, I've had the opportunity to meet some truly remarkable people: people who are working hard to overcome struggles to reach amazing goals. One characteristic that I've found to be consistent among all of these individuals is how clear they are about their goals. When asked what they are working

# GAIN Planning

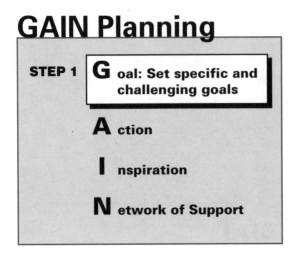

**STEP 1**  **G** oal: Set specific and challenging goals

**A** ction

**I** nspiration

**N** etwork of Support

towards, without hesitation, they can crisply and succinctly answer. They have no doubt about what their goals are, and I have no doubt that this clarity is a key factor in their success.

Another common characteristic shared by the successful people I've worked with and interviewed is that their goals are challenging. They have to learn new skills, take risks, and stretch themselves to the limits of their ability. I believe these challenges contribute to their resolve to succeed.

It takes wisdom and humility to emulate the successful practices of others. By following the lead of other successful people and crafting your goals to be more specific and challenging, you can dramatically increase your own potential for success.

## Dream Big

Life is full of opportunities! You are fortunate to be alive at a time when, with hard work and determination, you can be, have, or do almost anything you desire. So don't cheat yourself. Dream big dreams, wish big wishes, and hold the highest of hopes.

There is no reason you can't go to Rome, start your own business, become a doctor, buy your dream boat, climb Mt. Kilimanjaro, or write a best-selling book, if that's what you want to do. No matter what goals you choose, the process for reaching them is the same. So why not aim high and take advantage of all that life has to offer?

### WARNING
#### Set the Right Goals For You

Before I share a process with you that will dramatically increase your chances of achieving your goals, I need to warn you: THIS PROCESS WORKS. If you follow it, you will succeed. Why am I telling you this?

Consider these words of wisdom from Steven Covey, author of *The Seven Habits of Highly Successful People*:

**"When you are climbing the ladder of success, it is important to look up and make sure the ladder is leaning against the right building."**

In other words, be careful what you wish for.

Before you start creating GAIN Plans to reach your goals, you need to think seriously about what you really want in life. Setting and reaching significant goals requires sacrifices of time, energy, money, and the opportunity cost of not working on other goals. So before you continue, take a few minutes to answer the following questions:

- What makes me truly happy?
- What do I value most?
- What are my top three priorities?
- What do I enjoy doing?

Use your answers to these questions to guide your choices about what goals are right for you. If your goals won't make you happy, are out of alignment with your priorities, or run counter to what you value, it will be difficult for you to commit to them. And, if you do reach them, you may end up wondering why you set them in the first place.

# Set Specific Goals

Once your priorities are clear, you are ready to start setting goals. While your dreams should be expansive, your goals need to be specific. Break your big dreams down into specific goals that you can start working on today. Setting very specific goals allows you to focus your energy exclusively on tasks that will get you where you want to go. You can think of it as the difference between a floodlight and a laser beam. A laser beam cuts with unparalleled precision because all of its energy is focused tightly on one spot. When your goals are not specific, you run the risk of diffusing your energy in too many directions.

For example, if you dream of starting your own business, you may need to set a number of smaller, more specific goals in order to realize that dream. You may need to save a certain amount of money for start-up costs, go back to school to learn a new skill, or spend time creating a product you hope to sell. By breaking your dream of owning your own business into smaller parts, you can focus on each part at the appropriate time.

We've all had the experience of setting goals that were too broad. These goals often leave us frustrated and disappointed. Exercise and fitness goals tend to be prime culprits of overly broad goals. Have you ever set a goal such as, "I will lose weight" or "I will get into shape"?

What happened?

While these are worthy objectives, they are not specific enough for you to be able to create an action plan that guarantees your success.

Will you be happy if you lose two pounds, or five pounds, or twelve pounds? If you don't get winded climbing a flight of stairs have you met your goal of getting into shape? When will you know you have succeeded so you can take a break and celebrate your success?

To be able to measure your progress and celebrate your success, your goals need to be specific.

### Harness the Power of Words

Put your specific goals in writing. I can't overstate the importance of putting your goals into writing. It's an important step in solidifying your commitment to them. To ensure your goals are specific, write your goal statements using the first person active voice and wording that is as precise as possible.

Start each goal statement with "I will . . ." and state specifically what you will do. For example, instead of setting the goal, "Spend more time with my family," set the goal, "I will spend at least two evenings a week, and three Saturdays a month, with my spouse and children."

Specific goals help you zero in on your target. They also make it much easier to accurately judge your distance from it.

## Set Challenging Goals

Why set challenging goals? Wouldn't it be better to set easy goals?

Challenging goals stretch you to the limits of your abilities, and when you succeed, they expand your beliefs about what's possible. The more challenging your goals, the sweeter the taste of victory when you reach them.

## START EACH GOAL STATEMENT WITH "I WILL . . . "

Here are some examples of how you might rewrite some common goals to make them more specific.

### Specific Goal Examples

| NOT SPECIFIC | SPECIFIC |
|---|---|
| Lose weight | I will lose 12 pounds in four months. |
| Get into shape | I will exercise aerobically for at least 25 minutes four times per week. |
| Go to college | I will earn a college degree from a four year university. |
| Eat healthy | I will limit my caloric intake to 2000 or less calories per day, and I will eat 22 grams or less of saturated fat per day. |
| Earn more money | I will ask my manager for a 10 percent raise at my next performance review. |
| Find a new job | I will find a new job in [insert your field] with a medium to large company within 30 minutes of my house. |

### Specific Goals Exercise

Now you try it. Rewrite the following two goals to make them more specific.

1. Take a vacation this year.

_____

_____

2. Take up a hobby.

_____

_____

Did you write something like this?

1. I will take off two weeks in July and spend them in Florida with my family.

2. I will learn to play the piano and spend at least three hours per week practicing.

If so, then you've got the hang of it. From now on, whenever you set a goal, make sure it's specific. Doing so will dramatically increase your probability of succeeding.

Challenging goals also keep life interesting. They encourage you to think and grow in new and exciting ways. They tax you mentally and physically and, in the process, make you stronger and more confident.

**One's mind, once stretched by a new idea, never regains its original dimensions.**

*Oliver Wendell Homes*

Each time you set, and reach, a challenging goal, your confidence builds. You realize that you have a deep pool of untapped potential. This realization leads you to set even more challenging goals in the future. When this starts happening, you've begun an upward spiral towards success. Where that spiral ends is limited only by your imagination.

### What's the Right Challenge Level?

Imagine for a moment that you've just awakened in a strange place. You're not sure what town or even what state you're in. All you know is that your goal is to get to New York City as quickly as possible. How challenging will this goal be? When will you arrive? Should you drive, fly, or take the train?

These are impossible questions to answer, unless you can get the answer to one critical question: "Where are you right now?" The same is true of any goal. To accurately assess the challenge level of a goal, you need to determine where you're starting from. If your goal is to weigh 165 pounds and you're currently 210 pounds, this is a more challenging goal than if you weigh 175 pounds today.

Once you know where you're starting from, you have to consider the amount of time, energy, skill, and expense required to reach your goal. Identifying these factors will help you to realistically gauge the level of challenge your goal represents. The amount of time can be measured in daily, weekly, or monthly intervals. The amount of energy can be physical, mental, or both. The amount of skill should include whether or not you need to learn something new. The expense is obviously how much it will cost, which may or may not be an issue. The combination of these four factors: time, energy, skill, and expense, equals the challenge level of your goal. I call this formula the Challenge Level Equation.

## Challenge Level Equation

Time + Energy + Skill + Expense = Challenge Level

Based on your assessment of each challenge level factor, rank the challenge level of your goal from 1 to 5 using the scale below.

**5** = Most challenging    **4** = Very challenging    **3** = Challenging
**2** = Somewhat challenging    **1** = Not very challenging

When you set goals, you can use this equation to estimate how much challenge each goal represents. It is not an exact science, but rather a way to ensure you consider some of the important factors in your ability to reach your goals.

There's nothing wrong with setting easy goals along with your more challenging ones. In fact, it's a good idea to make some of your goals easier. By doing so, you get the chance to experience success often and have the opportunity to celebrate on a regular basis. In addition, you'll find that momentum is a very powerful force. Just like a sports team coming off a win, success with your easier goals will help propel you towards your more difficult ones. The trick is to find the right balance.

When you work on several different goals simultaneously, it's important that they have varying degrees of challenge. Too many challenging goals can lead to frustration, while too few can lead to apathy. Only you know what the right mix is at any given time. Whatever it is, being purposeful about what you choose to work towards is another key factor to your success.

By setting specific and challenging goals, you set yourself up for success. You have a clear destination and you know how difficult it will be to reach it.

*The first step in developing winning GAIN Plans is to set specific and challenging goals.*

---

**ATTENTION**

You've come to a critical choice point! You must decide whether you want to merely read this book or use it as a powerful tool for achieving your goals. What follows is the first of a number of opportunities you'll have to get to work setting goals and creating action plans to realize them. You can skip these sections and still get something out of the book. However, if you choose to exert the effort required to put these tools to work for you, you'll get exponentially more value out of your experience.

---

## Your GAIN Planning Tools

It's my sincere hope that you'll do more than just read this book. I'd love to see you use it as a tool for making positive things happen in your life. In that spirit, I encourage you to choose one important goal you would like to achieve and keep it in focus as you read on. After an explanation of each GAIN Planning step, I'll ask you to spend a few minutes working on a GAIN Plan for the goal you've selected. By the end of Part One, you will have a completed GAIN Plan for your goal. Let's start now.

Set the book aside for a few minutes and think about an important goal you would like to achieve. Be specific. Maybe you want to change careers, take the trip of a lifetime, or learn to scuba dive. The goal you choose should provide you with an appropriate amount of challenge. Make it something that will stretch you, but that you are confident you can achieve. Think about it now.

Write two or three potential specific and challenging goals below:

1. I will _____
2. I will _____
3. I will _____

When you complete the Goal portion of your GAIN Plan at the end of this section, you will notice three questions following the space where you write your goal statement. These questions are designed to ensure that you are crystal clear about your goal.

They are:

**1. How will success look and feel?**

It's important to visualize how reaching your goal will look and feel. For example, if your goal is to graduate from college, picture your graduation. What does the podium look like? What are you wearing (a cap and gown)? Who's there to see you receive your diploma? How does it feel to be there? There's clear evidence that people who clearly visualize achieving their goals are at an advantage over those who don't. Besides, it's fun to daydream!

# Quick Tips

## for Setting Specific and Challenging Goals

- Commit to the right goals for you
- Set specific, challenging, and tightly focused goals
- Start each goal statement with, "I will . . ."
- Set goals at the right challenge level
- Keep a balance of goals that present varying levels of challenge

**2. How will I measure my progress towards this goal?**

As I said earlier, it's critical that you have a way to measure your progress. Without the ability to do this, it's very difficult to stay motivated or to make necessary adjustments. For our goal of graduating from college, we could measure our progress by looking at the units we've taken, our grades, and how many credits we have outstanding.

**3. How will this goal stretch me beyond my current abilities?**

You need to know how your goals will stretch you. This allows you to keep an appropriate balance of challenge among your goals. It also gives you some insight into how your goals will enable you to grow.

It's time for you to take the first step in developing a winning GAIN Plan for one of your goals. Choose one goal from the options you listed on the previous page and fill out the Goal portion of your GAIN Plan on the next page.

# Step 1 GAIN Plan Form

**GOAL:** Set a specific and challenging goal.　　Date: _____

- Write your specific and challenging goal statement below. Begin with "I will . . ."

_____

_____

_____

- How will my success look and feel?

_____

_____

_____

- How will I measure my progress towards this goal?

_____

_____

_____

- How will this goal stretch me beyond my current abilities?

_____

_____

_____

Time + Energy + Skill + Expense = Challenge Level

***Rank the challenge level of this goal:*** Circle One Number

**5** = Most challenging　　**4** = Very challenging　　**3** = Challenging

**2** = Somewhat challenging　　**1** = Not very challenging

# Step 1 in Action

## You Can Do 26.2

*Believe you can, and you can!*

Norman Vincent Peale

It's hard to believe that a postcard could change your life. But, just like me, this is exactly what happens for many Team In Training athletes. The Leukemia & Lymphoma Society sends out over 5 million purple and green Team In Training promotional postcards each year. For many participants, this is their first introduction to the program. While the wording on the postcards differs, the offer is always the same. It states that, "Team In Training will help you reach your personal fitness goals, and pay your way to a race event, in exchange for your raising money for a cure. A cure to a disease that kills more children under age 15 than any other: leukemia. In addition, the money you raise will support research to cure other blood cancers, cancers that afflict more than 616,000 Americans."

It's an intriguing offer.

Intriguing enough to lure my wife Shari and me to that informational meeting back in 1998. We went mostly out of curiosity. That evening we learned all about how Team In Training works. We learned that anyone in good health who puts in the time, sweat, and energy involved in participating in the program can train to complete a marathon or other endurance event.

As we learned more about Team In Training and how successful it is, our interest deepened. Thoughts such as, "Well, maybe I could run a marathon," crept into our consciousness. Even so, committing to run a marathon is no small undertaking. The Team In Training program requires a huge investment of time and energy. Not only would we be training to compete in a taxing athletic event, we would simultaneously be working to raise a significant amount of money for charity.

 **Commit to the right goals for you**

Before we laced up our running shoes and signed up for the program, we wanted proof that Team In Training worked as well as the staff said it did, and that it was right for us.

That proof came from the Team In Training alumni speakers the first evening. We listened to a wide assortment of past Team In Training athletes. They varied in age, gender, body type, and background. Each stood in front of us in their purple and green Team In Training finishers jackets and shared their personal stories of transformation. They told us how, as a result of their participation in the program, they had completed their endurance race and had met, and in many cases exceeded, their minimum fundraising target. Standing with their finisher medals around their necks, beaming with pride, they talked about how Team In Training had impacted their lives. I decided that although I'd never considered running a marathon before, doing it with Team In Training would be the perfect opportunity. It would give me a chance to fulfill both fitness and altruistic goals. Shari and I signed up for the program that evening.

People join "the Team" for a wide variety of reasons: to get into better shape, to lose weight, to improve their nutrition, or because they've always dreamed of completing an endurance race and want professional training. Others want to meet new people or want the free travel to a race location. Some just want a new challenge. Whatever their reasons for joining, for many, the result of their participation is an unexpected transformation of mind and body. It was the question of how these peoples', and ultimately my own, transformations occurred that nagged at me after I completed the program.

I now realize that I got the first part of my answer to this question the night I signed up for the program.

 **Set specific, challenging, and tightly focused goals**

When I returned home after that first meeting, I sat down and read through my participant notebook. As I did, I was struck by the enormity of the task I had undertaken. I had committed to two significant goals. The first goal was to train for and complete the 1998 inaugural Suzuki Rock 'n' Roll Marathon in San Diego. This alone seemed daunting!

The second goal and, in retrospect, the far more important one, was to raise a minimum of $1,500 for The Leukemia & Lymphoma Society.

Looking back, I can see the beauty and effectiveness of these goals. Team In Training participants set goals that are specific, challenging, and tightly focused. For me, the goals were clear and could be stated in two compact sentences: "I will train to run 26.2 miles." And, "I will raise $1,500 for charity." These were targets I could continually gauge my distance from, both in mileage covered and dollars raised. They left no doubt about how I would measure my success.

Team In Training also helps participants break these two large goals down into smaller parts. The participant notebook has sections for both the endurance training and fundraising goals. Breaking them apart makes them less overwhelming. However, they are still quite challenging.

 **Set goals at the right challenge level**

The challenge level represented by each Team In Training participant's goals varies. For those in superior physical condition, the physical training is not very taxing. For them, it may be the fundraising that represents the biggest challenge. For others who may have extensive personal and professional networks, exceeding their fundraising target may be fairly easy. For them, it might be the endurance training that represents the biggest hurdle. For still others, an unanticipated injury or other life event might increase their challenge level. Some of the most impressive participants in the program are blood cancer patients themselves. They are either in remission or have beaten their diseases. Joining Team In Training as athletes gives them the opportunity to train for, and complete, an endurance race that would have been impossible in the midst of their illnesses. In the process, they raise money to find a cure for the very diseases that have afflicted them. You will learn more about how these amazing individuals overcame some seemingly insurmountable challenges when you read their stories in Part Two.

 **Keep a balance of goals that present varying levels of challenge**

Team In Training ensures that the program's fitness and fundraising goals are appropriately challenging. A nice aspect of Team In Training goals is that you can adjust them to make sure they represent a balance of challenge levels. If simply completing your endurance race isn't challenging enough, you can set a goal for a specific time. And if the fundraising minimum, in your estimation, isn't challenging enough, you can set a personal goal that far exceeds it, as many participants have done. Later, you will hear stories shared by people who have raised in excess of $100,000. While your Team In Training goals are sure to stretch your fitness, endurance, and fundraising stamina, they are not beyond reach. Team In Training goals are exactly the kind of specific and challenging goals you might set as part of a GAIN Plan. They are also the first key to the program's success.

As an example, let's assume you have signed up as a Team In Training participant for the 2004 Suzuki Rock 'n' Roll Marathon in San Diego. Here's how the Goal portion of your GAIN Plan might look:

# Sample Step 1 GAIN Plan Form

**GOAL:** Set a specific and challenging goal.     Date: _2/1/04_

- Write your specific and challenging goal statement below.
  Begin with "I will . . . "

  _I will train for and complete the Suzuki Rock 'n' Roll_
  _Marathon in San Diego, in June of 2004._

- How will my success look and feel?

  _I can close my eyes and see myself crossing the finish line and_
  _having a finisher's medal hung around my neck. I can also_
  _imagine the pride I will feel in meeting this goal._

- How will I measure my progress towards this goal?

  _I can measure my progress daily in mileage run._

- How will this goal stretch me beyond my current abilities?

  _If simply finishing the race is not challenging enough, I can_
  _raise the bar by attempting to complete my race at a certain_
  _pace._

Time + Energy + Skill + Expense = Challenge Level

**Rank the challenge level of this goal:** Circle One Number

**5** = Most challenging     **④**= Very challenging     **3** = Challenging
**2** = Somewhat challenging     **1** = Not very challenging

You would complete a separate GAIN Plan for reaching your fundraising goal.

---

# Create Detailed and Realistic Action Plans

*Even if you are on the right track, you'll get run over if you just sit there.*

Will Rogers

Earlier, I encouraged you to dream big dreams and from those dreams to set specific and challenging goals. Once you do this, though, the task of accomplishing these goals can seem overwhelming. At times you may feel like you are at the bottom of a mountain whose peak you can't see. You may even question the wisdom of attempting to climb to such lofty heights. It's at this point that the need for a solid action plan comes to light.

The best way to curb any self-doubt you harbor is to channel your energy into making plans for reaching the summit. Use your apprehension as a powerful motivator. It's the most productive thing you can do.

Maybe for you it isn't apprehension, but procrastination, or having too much on your plate. Whatever it is that's kept you from reaching your goals in the past, creating detailed and realistic action plans is part of the solution.

Beyond setting specific and challenging goals, the successful individuals and teams I've worked with have solid action plans. They outline the steps they need to take and determine how and when they will take them. This methodical approach is important, considering how much the pace of our lives has quickened. We're all trying to do more with less and in the process

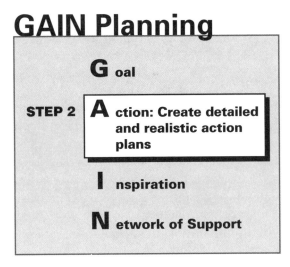

# GAIN Planning

**G** oal

**STEP 2** | **A** ction: Create detailed and realistic action plans

**I** nspiration

**N** etwork of Support

we're stretching ourselves exceedingly thin. In order to reach the summits we're attempting, we must have solid action plans for getting there.

Step two in the GAIN Planning process is to create detailed and realistic action plans for reaching your specific and challenging goals. Step two is critical because it's the point in the process where your dreams are transformed from abstract hopes into concrete plans. Even so, many people find action planning to be the hardest aspect of GAIN Planning. It lacks the excitement of the starting line (setting your goal) and the triumph of the finish line (reaching your goal). But, action planning is the hard work, the perspiration, that gets you from the starting line to the finish line.

## Develop Written Action Plans

The act of writing out your action plans in detail—not just thinking about them—is important. Your challenging goals often require you to take many individual steps in order to reach your destination. With all the competing priorities in your life, it's easy to get sidetracked. Writing out your action plans will help you keep your attention and energy focused on the tasks that will get you where you want to go.

Here's a list of what each of your action plans will need to include:

- A specific target completion date
- A detailed list of the tasks you will complete to reach your goal and when you will complete them

- A list of any obstacles that may inhibit you from reaching your goal
- A plan for overcoming these obstacles

## Establish Target Completion Dates

Identifying target completion dates for your goals is one of the best ways to combat procrastination. Let's face it, while goal-related activities may be in your best interest, they're not always the most exciting. When you have a specific target completion date for each of your goals it helps you to hold yourself accountable to meeting your deadlines. As your target dates draw nearer, your motivation increases.

Once you determine where you are starting from with your goals, you should be able to accurately estimate when you will reach them. It's critical, though, that you take into account all of the competing priorities in your life. Think back to what you identified as your priorities in Step 1. How does each goal fit with those priorities? You may want to fast-track those goals that are higher on your priority list and give yourself more time for those that are of lower priority.

Make your target completion date for each goal realistic; you'll need to work backwards from that date to plan the tasks required to meet that goal. Also, try not to get too frustrated if you have to adjust your target to a later date. It's not unusual to encounter additional tasks or unexpected obstacles that require such an adjustment. Likewise, there may be times when you actually overestimate how long it will take to meet your target. On these occasions, you may need to revise your target to an earlier date!

## List Specific Tasks

Once you've set your target completion date, you're ready to list the specific tasks you'll need to accomplish to meet it. Write down each of these tasks and include an accompanying completion date. The GAIN Planning forms in Part Three will make this a snap.

Writing out all of these tasks may seem like overkill, but it serves two important purposes. It forces you to sit down and think about what you must do—specifically. And, as you write your list, you'll find that additional tasks come to mind, things you might have overlooked had you not taken the time to write out each task.

In some cases, you may not be sure of everything you need to do to reach your goal. When this happens, you'll need to do some research. Use all the resources at your disposal, including books, the Internet, other people, and anything else you need. People who have accomplished the same or similar goals can be great resources.

Don't forget to identify the knowledge and skills you'll need to develop in order to reach your goal. You will want to set tasks for gaining those important resources as well.

## Celebrate Your Progress

The goals you set are your destinations. The specific tasks you identify to get you to your destinations are the mile-markers that will line your path. They're important because they give you feedback about your progress. Your completed tasks let you know you're moving in the right direction and making headway. You'd be wise to celebrate the passing of each mile-marker, because it's a clear sign that you are one step closer to your goal.

If you're like me, though, you may at times get so focused on reaching your destination that you miss the scenery and the opportunities for celebrations along the way. I call these celebrations along the way "in-route" celebrations.

In-route celebrations are about celebrating your progress, not just your arrival. They are about giving yourself

**Detailed and realistic action plans allow you to measure your progress and celebrate your journey!**

credit for the hard work you are putting into reaching your goals and recognizing that life is blazing by at a frightening pace and that you need to celebrate what you have and what you've accomplished every day. Besides, each step you take towards your goals is a learning experience. Hopefully your challenging goals are in alignment with your overall hopes and dreams. When they are, your journey towards them becomes a constant learning experience. You can continually ask yourself, "What's working? What's not? How can I improve? How can I apply what I've learned to my other goals?" What you learn from answering these questions alone is cause for celebration.

# Identify Potential Obstacles and Create Plans to Overcome Them

No matter how good your action plans are or how much you learn from your progress, you are bound to encounter some obstacles along the path to your goals. The more challenging your goals, the larger the obstacles you will likely face. Taking time upfront to consider the obstacles that may impede your progress will help you formulate a plan to overcome them.

As you think about the obstacles you may face, you will find that they can often be divided into two categories: goal-related obstacles and personality-related obstacles. Just like they sound, goal-related obstacles have more to do with the nature of your goal while personality-related obstacles have more to do with your personality traits.

### *Goal-Related Obstacles*

Recently, one of the managers I was coaching set the following goal: "I will spend at least 30 minutes a month with each of my employees one-on-one. In these meetings I will provide them with positive and developmental feedback as well as answer any questions they have for me."

After setting this goal, I asked her to consider some of the goal-related obstacles that might get in her way of succeeding.

Here's one of a few she identified:

- **Lack of time to prepare** (With 14 employees, preparing for these meetings seemed overwhelming).

Having anticipated this goal-related obstacle, we proactively created a plan to overcome it.

Here's what we came up with:

- **Lack of time to prepare:** I suggested she carry a micro-cassette recorder to record her thoughts and feedback during the month as she interacted with her employees. She did this, as well as had her assistant type and organize her thoughts before her meetings. This solution worked quite well for her.

## Personality-Related Obstacles

Beyond the obstacles inherent in the nature of your goal, some of the obstacles you will encounter have more to do with your personality. As you review your action plans, think about which tasks will be hardest for you due to the nature of your personality.

Are you someone who procrastinates? Do you find it difficult to stay focused on one thing? Do you tend to start too quickly and burn out before you reach the end? Are you shy, but your goal requires you to meet new people? Knowing the answers to questions such as these will help you create action plans that are realistic for you.

For example, if you're not a morning person, don't include getting up at 5:00 A.M. to study as part of your action plan for going back to school. It would be better to plan your study sessions at times when you know you'll have the most energy.

By considering both the goal-related and personality-related obstacles you may face, you are better prepared for them when they arise. In addition, you will have more energy to deal with the unanticipated obstacles you are sure to encounter.

### Quick Tips

**for Creating Detailed and Realistic Action Plans**

- Develop written action plans
- Establish target completion dates
- Determine what you need to do on a daily, weekly, and monthly basis to reach your goals
- Celebrate your progress
- Consider the obstacles you may face and develop a plan to overcome them
- Remain flexible
- Review and revise your action plans regularly

## Remain Flexible and Revise Regularly

Do your best to always set yourself up for success! While your goals should challenge you, your action plans need to be realistic. A key ingredient to being realistic is flexibility. You may need to adjust your time frame, add additional steps, or account for unexpected obstacles. You should take time to review and revise your action plans regularly. It helps to think of your action plans as being fluid. They need to adjust to your changing circumstances and priorities.

Most importantly, don't underestimate your abilities. You have tremendous potential to make positive things happen in your life. Challenge yourself to create action plans that will get you where you want to go as fast as reasonably possible.

*The second step in developing winning GAIN Plans is to create detailed and realistic action plans.*

## Your GAIN Planning Tools

Think back to the goal you identified on page 22. What tasks do you need to complete to accomplish this goal? What obstacles might you encounter? How will you overcome those obstacles? Write your answers to these questions in the Action Plan portion of your GAIN Plan on the following page.

# Step 2 G*A*IN Plan Form

**A**CTION PLAN: Create a detailed and realistic action plan.

Target Completion Date: _____

| Task | Date/On-Going |
|------|---------------|
| 1. _____ | |
| 2. _____ | |
| 3. _____ | |
| 4. _____ | |
| 5. _____ | |
| 6. _____ | |
| 7. _____ | |
| 8. _____ | |

**Obstacles that may inhibit me . . .**

_____

_____

**I will overcome these obstacles by . . .**

_____

_____

❑ **Target completion date and tasks written in calendar.**

As you make progress towards your goal, shade in the approximate percentage completed.

| | | | | |
|---|---|---|---|---|
| 0 | 25 | 50 | 75 | 100 |

# Step 2 in Action

## Put One Foot in Front of the Other

*The fight is won or lost far away from witnesses—behind the lines, in the gym and out there on the road, long before I dance under those lights.*

Muhammad Ali

Team In Training's participants have a very high success rate of meeting their fitness and fundraising goals. This success rate can largely be attributed to the program's exceptional ability to help diverse groups of people create detailed and realistic action plans to meet their goals.

When Shari and I recovered from the initial shock of the Team In Training goals we had committed to, we got to work figuring out how we were going to reach them. We learned that Team In Training was well equipped to help us—and every other participant who joins—create an action plan that all but guarantees success.

**Develop written action plans**

The quality of the action plans Team In Training helps its participants create can largely be credited to the program's impressive coaching staff. Comprised of over 800 coaches, Team In Training has more coaches than all the U.S. professional sports teams combined. These coaches design, coordinate, and monitor all of the participant training for race events. They are spread out among The Leukemia & Lymphoma Society's 60 chapters and many are world-class athletes themselves. Between the binder each athlete receives and the customization from the coaching staff, every athlete begins the program with a clear action plan.

 **Establish target completion dates**

When you join Team In Training you join a team that is training for a specific race. The date of your race is used to establish your training schedule, fundraising deadlines, and many other aspects of your preparation. This ensures that participants have adequate time to prepare for their event.

 **Determine what you need to do on a daily, weekly, and monthly basis to reach your goals**

Shari and I quickly realized that our Team In Training participant binder was more than just a resource: it was our training and fundraising bible. It told us, specifically, what we needed to do to achieve our goals. It was the foundation of our action plan.

Here is an abbreviated list of some of the invaluable resources we found in our binder:

- Important target dates and deadlines
- Detailed training schedules
- Nutrition basics
- Stretching guidelines
- Injury prevention tips
- Equipment selection guidance
- Fundraising suggestions

- Sample fundraising letters

Shari and I relied heavily on our binder throughout our training. We referred to it daily for training distances, nutritional suggestions, new stretches, fundraising suggestions, and many other helpful tips. In addition, the coaching staff worked with us to customize our training regimen to fit our endurance levels.

When participants join Team In Training, they tend to focus first on creating an action plan to reach their fitness goals. They want to know how the race training works. Common questions include, "What will my training consist of?" "How far will I have to run, bike, or swim each week?" And, "How often will I need to work out?"

## Endurance Race Training

The length of your training program is determined by the race for which you're preparing. In 2002, more than 30,000 Team In Training athletes competed in over 50 accredited endurance races in the U.S. and abroad. The average training period for these races was four to five months.

Team In Training began as a marathon training program, and though it has grown to include other sports, marathon training is still the largest component of the program. By looking at Team In Training's running program, you can get a clear picture of how the endurance training works for all of the sports.

As a marathon team participant, your goal is to be physically and mentally prepared to either run or walk 26.2 miles. While in the program, you run on your own during the week. On weekends you join your team for group training sessions. These sessions are organized and supported by Team In Training staff and volunteers.

The distances start short and build over time. As an added benefit, the weekend group runs are held in various locations around the city in which you are training. This gives you a chance to run in new and interesting locations.

The coaching staff provides participants with weekly training schedules detailing how far to run each day, when to take days off, and when to cross train (do some exercise other than running).

 **Celebrate your progress**

One of the beautiful aspects of Team In Training is that it's nearly impossible not to celebrate your progress on a weekly basis. A big part of the group training sessions is support, encouragement, and celebration. As you pass personal endurance milestones and new distance mile-markers, you have friends, coaches, and mentors to help you celebrate your progress. Shari and I looked forward to reaching our weekly milestones because we knew a celebration with our teammates was bound to ensue.

 **Consider the obstacles you may face and develop a plan to overcome them**

No matter how diligent you are with your training regimen, there is little doubt that you will face obstacles when preparing for a marathon. Some will be goal-related (an injury that forces you to cut back your training distances) and others personality-related (the difficulty of waking up at 5:00 A.M. to run before work). Every participant is made aware of these types of potential obstacles, obstacles that include the risks of under-training, over-training, poor nutrition, dehydration, injury, and procrastination. This is also why your marathon training consists of much more than just running. You are educated about every aspect of the sport, with readings and clinics on subjects such as injury prevention, form, technique, nutrition, equipment selection, and race strategy.

**Currently, one out of every 15 U.S. marathon runners participates through Team In Training.**

 **Remain flexible**

The marathon training is extremely well organized and professionally run. If you stick to the training regimen, by the end, you will be well prepared to run, or walk, your marathon. There's enough flexibility built into the program to account for the challenges participants face. The Team In Training coaching staff proudly points out that the endurance training plan has been road-tested by more than 150,000 past participants. Put quite simply, they will tell you, "It works!"

# Fundraising

What also works is the fundraising component of Team In Training. Once participants are confident they will be physically prepared for their race, they usually turn their attention to the fundraising. They want to know, "How much will I have to raise?" and "How will I raise it?"

When you join Team In Training, in exchange for training, education, organized group runs, travel, accommodations, and race entry fees, you are obligated to raise a minimum amount of money for The Leukemia & Lymphoma Society. The amount varies depending on the duration of your training and the cost of travel and accommodations to your race event. With events held in many beautiful locations including Honolulu, HI, San Diego, CA, Spokane, WA, and Dublin, Ireland, this is a pretty good deal.

So how do Team In Training participants raise the required funds? In every way imaginable! From garage sales to silent auctions, from raffles to bake sales to pancake breakfasts. There are countless other creative strategies as well. However, the majority of funds are raised through letter writing campaigns. This is the process of making a list of everyone you know and then sending each person on your list a fundraising letter. In the letter you explain that you are being trained to compete in an endurance race and in exchange are raising funds for The Leukemia & Lymphoma Society.

Many Team In Training participants are astonished by the effectiveness of their letter writing campaigns. They often learn that they have friends and relatives who are close to people afflicted with a blood cancer. The amount and sources of their donations often surprise participants.

Team In Training provides you with everything you need to write a fundraising letter that's sure to generate a big response.

Anyone who questions the effectiveness of these letter writing campaigns need look no further than the program's top two individual fundraisers.

While training for the 1998 Suzuki Rock 'n' Roll Marathon, Anthony Iacono of Secaucus, NJ, set a Team In Training fundraising record, raising more than $100,000 in honor of his son, Paul. He didn't stop there. Since becoming involved, Anthony has raised more than $200,000 for The Leukemia & Lymphoma Society, primarily through letter writing campaigns. You can find Anthony and his son Paul's inspiring story entitled "The Entertainer" in Part Two, on page 134.

Believing that these types of fundraising records are made to be broken, Iacono was pleased to see his record surpassed the following year by John Kellenyi of Maplewood, NJ. While training and fundraising for the 1999 Marine Corps Marathon in Washington D.C., Kellenyi raised $121,000 through his letter writing campaign. The following year Kellenyi broke his own record, raising $144,000 while training for the 2000 Mardi Gras Marathon in New Orleans in memory of his friend Jay McCabe.

Although they don't know one another, Anthony Iacono and John Kellenyi have collectively raised more than $465,000 in the past five years. Their success makes the effectiveness of Team In Training's letter writing campaigns indisputable. Both Iacono and Kellenyi plan to continue fundraising for future events. Even so, they hope that their records will continue to be surpassed!

Team In Training athletes receive all the resources they need to create detailed and realistic action plans to meet their endurance training and fundraising goals. These action plans are exactly the type of action plans you might create as part of an effective GAIN Plan.

Returning to our 2004 Suzuki Rock 'n' Roll Marathon example, here's how the Action Plan portion of your GAIN Plan might look:

# Sample Step 2 G*A*IN Plan Form

**A**CTION PLAN: Create a detailed and realistic action plan.

Target Completion Date: _June 2004_

| **Task** | **Date/On-going** |
|---|---|
| 1. *Join the San Diego Chapter of Team In Training* | *January 2004* |
| 2. *Review and follow the participant's training manual* | *Ongoing* |
| 3. *Attend all scheduled group runs* | *Ongoing* |
| 4. *Follow the provided weekday workout schedule* | *Ongoing* |
| 5. *Learn and follow the training nutritional guidelines* | *Ongoing* |
| 6. *Buy recommended shoes and running apparel* | *January 2004* |
| 7. *Read and implement tips for avoiding injury* | *January 2004* |
| 8. *Find a running partner in my area* | *January 2004* |

**Obstacles that may inhibit me . . .**

*The potential of an injury, my tendency to procrastinate, and dehydration.*

**I will overcome these obstacles by . . .**

*Following the guidelines in my binder for injury prevention, identifying a running buddy*

*who'll keep me from procrastinating, and drinking lots of water on my training runs.*

❑ **Target completion date and tasks written in calendar.**

As you make progress towards your goal, shade in the approximate percentage completed.

| 0 | 25 | 50 | 75 | 100 |
|---|---|---|---|---|

# S T E P 3

## Identify Compelling Inspirations

*Inspiration ignites and sustains action.*

Once you've set specific and challenging goals and have taken the time to create detailed and realistic action plans, how can you be sure that you will stay motivated until you achieve your goals? By clearly identifying and tapping into your compelling inspirations. The definition of inspiration is *an animating action or influence*, literally something that compels a person to move or act. In the case of your goals, your inspirations are what force you to stay the course no matter what obstacles you face.

When I work with individuals and teams, I often ask them to reflect on goals they've set that they never completed. When we look at why they failed to reach these goals, we often find a common theme. They failed at goals they were never motivated to reach in the first place. Maybe it was something their spouse, parent, team leader, or boss wanted them to do, but it was not important to them. They simply were not inspired to

# GAIN Planning

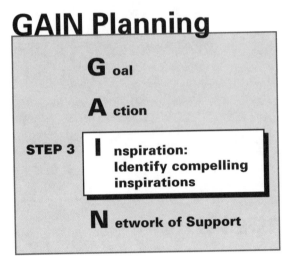

put in the effort required to reach the goal. Think about goals you've failed to reach. Were you uninspired by some of them? Most likely, yes.

This is why it's so important to set goals that are in alignment with what's truly important to you. When you do, identifying and tapping into your inspiration is easy.

## The Spark That Ignites Your Desire

Your inspiration for completing some of your goals is obvious. It may even be the spark that ignites your desire to set the goal in the first place. For example, what would you do to help your child if he or she were struck with a deadly cancer? If you don't have children, insert spouse, parent, sibling, or friend where it says child. What would you do to save your own life? In all likelihood, you would answer "almost anything" to both questions. Your answers confirm what you probably already know. You would be very inspired to do anything to save the life of a loved one or your own life.

In most cases, though, your inspiration for working toward a goal won't be as clear as in these examples. You may have to scratch below the surface to find what will sustain your motivation. I assure you, it's worth the effort. With so many competing priorities, you must be truly inspired in order to commit the time, energy, and resources required to reach your challenging goals.

## Your True Inspiration

Your inspiration is your answer to the question, "Why am I working towards this challenging goal in the first place? "

Your initial answer is not always your true inspiration. Let's say, for example, you have set a goal to find a better job. If I ask you why you've set this goal you might answer, "Because I want to make more money."

While there's certainly nothing wrong with making more money, this may not be your true inspiration. To get at your true inspiration, I might imitate a young child and keep asking, "Why? Why do you want to make more money?" "So I can provide a more comfortable lifestyle for my family," you might answer.

"Why do you want to provide a more comfortable lifestyle for your family?" "Because I love them and it makes me happy to see them enjoying the benefits of a more comfortable lifestyle."

Now we have tapped into your true inspiration. You want to find a better job so you can provide the benefits of a more comfortable lifestyle to the people you love. This is a more compelling inspiration than simply making more money. When your job hunt becomes difficult, you can picture your family enjoying the benefits of a more comfortable lifestyle and reinvigorate your search.

Participants in my training programs are sometimes annoyed when I ask them, "Why have you set that goal?" Often I will ask them "Why?" three to five more times. What I've found is that by the third or fourth "Why," they are getting closer to their true inspiration. When this happens, something clicks and they understand the reason for my questioning. I encourage you to use this same tactic with yourself. Whenever you set a goal, ask yourself, "Why" as I did in the above example until you get to your true inspiration.

## You Can Find Inspiration Anywhere

Think back to some of the goals you've set in the past but never completed. How inspired by them were you? Probably not very. When I work with individuals and teams in a business context, I often find that a lack of inspiration is at the root of many performance and morale problems.

I'm convinced that if we can help people find inspiration in their work, whatever it is, we'll have far fewer problems and a great deal more success. When I share this belief, I sometimes get questions such as, "How can I get excited about answering the phone all day, processing invoices, typing letters, etc.?" You can—by connecting what you're doing to the bigger picture. The key here is that you must believe in the work of the organization to which you belong. If you do, finding inspiration is easy. Just figure out how what you do is having a positive impact on the overall good of the organization. If you're answering the phone, processing invoices, or typing letters that are contributing to a company that provides a product or service you believe in, then you and your work are important. If you don't believe in what the organization is doing, you might consider moving on, because it's unlikely that you'll ever be inspired to give your all.

## Internal vs. External Inspiration

You may find that you have multiple inspirations for reaching many of your goals. That is, when you ask yourself why you want what you want, you may come up with a number of solid answers. That's fantastic! As you start to look at these inspirations, you're likely to find that they fall into two primary categories: internal inspirations and external inspirations.

Our inspiration to take on a challenging goal can be internal, external, or both. In the prior example about finding a new job, the inspiration is primarily external. It is your desire to create a more comfortable life for your family. There is an internal component as well: the satisfaction you know you'll feel when you create that lifestyle for your family.

It's important to know whether your inspiration is internal, external, or both. Knowing helps you determine where you will need to turn when your batteries are low and need to be recharged. If your inspiration is primarily internal, you may need to spend some quiet time alone thinking about why you are working on a particular goal. If your inspiration is primarily external, you may want to reconnect with what inspired you to take on your goal in the first place.

A combination of both internal and external inspiration is most powerful, but either is enough to sustain you, as long as it is compelling.

## Compelling Inspiration

How do you know if your inspiration for reaching your goal is compelling enough to sustain you until you succeed? To answer this, you need to determine just how motivated you are by the inspiration you have identified. The following scale should help you make this determination. When you set a goal and identify your inspiration, ask yourself and honestly answer:

**How motivated am I by the inspiration I have identified?**
Circle One Number

**5** = Extremely motivated    **4** = Very motivated    **3** = Motivated
**2** = Somewhat motivated    **1** = Not very motivated

If your answer is less than 3, reconsider setting this goal.
If your answer is 3 or higher, go for it!

If you can honestly answer 3, 4, or 5 then you've identified a compelling inspiration that should sustain you. If you answer 1 or 2 you need to look for a more compelling inspiration or consider postponing your goal until you're more inspired to work on it. One other thing—your inspiration needs to be correlated with the challenge level of your goal. If you set an extremely challenging goal, you will need to identify an extremely compelling inspiration. For example, if your goal is to run a marathon, the fact that a friend ran one is probably not going to be inspiring enough to give you that extra push when you most need it. On the other hand, running in honor of a cancer stricken family member or friend probably will be inspiring enough.

Knowing your true inspiration allows you to tap into your mental and physical reserves. It keeps you going when your motivation dips. The stronger your inspiration, the more powerful its ability to sustain you until you succeed.

## Compelling Inspiration Examples

| SPECIFIC GOAL | COMPELLING INSPIRATION |
| --- | --- |
| I will exercise aerobically for at least 25 minutes four times per week. | My inspiration for reaching this goal is that I know it will help me live a longer and healthier life and give me more time with the people I love. *Internal & External* |
| I will earn a college degree from a four year university. | My inspiration for reaching this goal is my burning desire to become the most educated and successful person I can be. *Primarily Internal* |

| Specific Goal | Compelling Inspiration |
|---|---|
| I will ask my manager for a 10 percent raise at my next performance review. | My inspiration for reaching this goal is that the extra money will allow me to save for my children's education, which is very important to me. |
| | *Internal & External* |
| I will find a new job in [insert your field] with a medium to large company within 30 minutes of my house. | My inspiration for reaching this goal is my desire to spend more time with my family. Cutting my commute to 30 minutes will give me an extra seven hours a week at home. |
| | *Primarily External* |

# Connect with Your Inspiration Daily

Once you've identified your true inspiration, you have a powerful motivating force at your disposal. To harness that force, you'll want to find ways to stay connected to it every day. Can it be captured in a photograph, poem, song, collage, or a note you write to yourself? The more tangible you can make your inspiration, the more power you give it to keep you moving forward.

The best large-scale example I've seen of this is the Team In Training hospital bracelet every athlete receives on which the name of the cancer patient for whom they are training is inscribed. The bracelet is an extremely effective physical connection between the athlete and at least one of their inspirations for training so hard.

Another example is something that Anthony Iacono (whose story you will read in Part Two) did after his son Paul's leukemia went into remission. When Paul completed his cancer treatment, an implanted port in his chest, used to deliver medication and chemotherapy intravenously during his treatment, was removed. Anthony took some of the tubing from the port and made a necklace from it. He wears the necklace as a constant reminder and inspiration to enjoy every day and to continue the fight for a cure to the cancer that unsuccessfully attempted to take his son.

If your goal doesn't lend itself to a hospital bracelet or medical port tubing, that's okay. Find something that fits. Maybe your inspiration for getting into better cardiovascular shape is that you want to be able to play with your children in the park without getting winded. If so, put a picture of your children in your wallet. Whenever you're considering "blowing off" a workout, pull out the photo and take a long hard look at it. Let your children's smiling faces give you the incentive to work out even when you don't feel like it.

## Quick Tips

### for Identifying Compelling Inspirations

- Identify your true inspiration
- You can find inspiration anywhere
- Make sure your inspiration is compelling
- Connect with your inspiration daily
- Share your inspiration with others

## Share Your Inspiration with Others

Sharing what inspires you is another great way to keep it ever-present. Let your friends, family members, coworkers, and others know about the journey you are taking towards your goals. Tell them what has inspired you to work so hard for what you want. When the people around you understand your goals and your inspirations, it raises the bar for your performance. It can also have the added benefit of inspiring other people to go for their dreams.

*The third step in developing winning GAIN Plans is to identify compelling inspirations.*

## Your GAIN Planning Tools

Think about the goal you identified on page 22. What is your true inspiration for reaching this goal? Can you clearly picture your inspiration? Is your inspiration compelling enough to enable you to overcome any obstacles that get in your way? Once you can answer "Yes" to all of these questions, write your compelling inspiration in the Inspiration portion of your GAIN Plan on the following page. Also, indicate what you'll use as a tangible connection to your goal (i.e., a photo, memento, note to yourself, etc.).

# Step 3 GA*I*N Plan Form

*I*NSPIRATION: Identify your compelling Inspiration.

**My true inspiration for reaching this goal is:**

_____

_____

_____

_____

**Then ask yourself:**

- Have I identified my true inspiration for working towards this goal?
- Can I clearly picture my inspiration for reaching this goal?

  I see . . . _____

  _____

  _____

  _____

**What will be my tangible connection to my inspiration?**

_____

_____

**How motivated am I by the inspiration I have identified?**
Circle One Number

　　　**5** = Extremely motivated　　**4** = Very motivated　　**3** = Motivated

　　　　　**2** = Somewhat motivated　　**1** = Not very motivated

If your answer is less than 3, reconsider setting this goal.
If your answer is 3 or higher, go for it!

# Step 3 in Action

## The Magic Ingredient

*It's always too early to quit.*

Norman Vincent Peale

The goals and action plans Team In Training helps you establish are central to each participant's success. But providing inspiration is the program's true magic ingredient. Team In Training is masterful at helping its participants identify multiple sources of internal and external inspirations for reaching their ambitious athletic and fundraising goals.

For Shari and me, it was purely inspiration that got us out of bed at 6:00 A.M. every Saturday morning to tax ourselves physically and mentally on the group training runs. It was also inspiration that motivated us to do the extra fundraising required to exceed our goal.

**TIP** → **Identify your true inspiration**

When people join Team In Training, their inspirations vary. For many these inspirations include the satisfaction they know they'll feel in pushing themselves to the limits of their physical and mental abilities. Others are inspired by the desire to visit a new and exciting place. Still others want to lose weight, get into better cardiovascular shape, or support a friend or loved one who's doing the program. These inspirations vary in importance to each participant. For some, it's the most important thing they're doing in their life. For others, it's just one of many things they are undertaking.

**Every five minutes, someone in the United States learns that he or she has leukemia, Hodgkin or non-Hodgkin lymphoma, or myeloma—that's more than 300 people a day.**

Quite possibly, the most inspired people in the program, at the outset, are those who have a child, spouse, sibling, or other loved one who has beaten, is battling, or has succumbed to a blood cancer. They know firsthand the ravages of the diseases they are raising money to cure, and they have very personal reasons for wanting those cures to be found quickly. But, for the majority of new Team In Training participants, including Shari and me, blood cancer is something of a mystery. This changes as soon as you join the program. Like every Team In Training athlete, Shari and I got quite an education about blood cancers as part of our Team In Training experience. What we learned solidified our commitment to working for a cure.

Here is just some of what we learned:

**Leukemia, Hodgkin and non-Hodgkin lymphoma,** and **myeloma** are cancers that originate in the bone marrow and lymphatic tissues. All cancers have two features in common: they start in a cell that is abnormal because of altered DNA and they contain cells that accumulate in excessive amounts.

Leukemia, Hodgkin and non-Hodgkin lymphoma, and myeloma are considered to be related cancers because they involve the uncontrolled growth of cells with similar functions and origins. The diseases result from an acquired genetic injury to the DNA of a single cell, which becomes abnormal (malignant) and multiplies continuously. The accumulation of these malignant cells interferes with the body's production of healthy

---

Blood cancer facts excerpted with permission from The Leukemia & Lymphoma Society's "Facts 2002."

blood cells and can leave the body unable to protect itself against infection.

**Every nine minutes, another child or adult is expected to die from leukemia, lymphoma, or myeloma. This is 165 people each day, or seven people every hour.**

In 2002, an estimated 106,300 people in the United States were diagnosed with leukemia, lymphoma, or myeloma. New cases of leukemia, Hodgkin and non-Hodgkin lymphoma, and myeloma accounted for 8.3 percent of the 1,284,900 new cancer cases diagnosed in the United States in 2002.

Leukemia, lymphoma, and myeloma caused the deaths of an estimated 58,300 people in the United States in 2002. These blood cancers accounted for nearly 10.5 percent of the deaths from cancer in 2002 based on the total of 555,500 cancer-related deaths. Leukemia is the leading cause of cancer death in women under the age of 20. Leukemia and lymphoma are the leading fatal cancers in young men under the age of 35.

 **Make sure your inspiration is compelling**

While these statistics are staggering, in many cases, it is the plight of blood cancer's youngest sufferers that drives Team In Training participants to far exceed their fundraising minimums. Leukemia is still the number one disease killer of children under age 15. This is the case even though the death rate from leukemia in children has declined by 61 percent in the past 30 years.

The stories in Part Two, by people who have experienced life with cancer, will help you begin to understand its harsh realities. But to understand the source of the inspiration that drives so many people to work so hard, to raise so much money, you must know that these realities are grim. They include: chemotherapy, blood transfusions, painful procedures, painful operations, pain in general, compromised immune systems, nausea, hair loss, extended hospital stays, isolation, loneliness, depression, grief, and countless other physical and emotional hardships. These are hardships no adult should have to endure, but for this to happen to a child is too unjust for words.

My personal experience with childhood cancer patients continually confirms this for me. For the past three years I've used our family's black Labrador Retriever, Jake, as a K-9 therapy dog. We visit Children's Hospital

**The leukemia death rate for children in the United States has declined 61 percent over the last three decades.**

in San Diego once a month so Jake can bring smiles to the faces of the children. Our visits to the pediatric oncology ward are always the most difficult, and the most rewarding. We go into each room and sit at the patient's bedside. If they are not too sick or too weak, they pet Jake and we talk about him and his amusing antics—like the time he ate a professionally decorated wedding cake when no one was looking. The kids are always most amused to hear that I reward Jake with McDonald's cheeseburgers that we get at the drive-thru on our way home.

To sit with these children, who are often bald and underweight, and talk to them as they smile and laugh through their pain is to understand the true meaning of COURAGE. It is their courage and the hope of finding a cure for their diseases that explains Team In Training's unmatched success.

# Treatment Breakthroughs

The good news and further inspiration for Team In Training athletes is that, through research over the past 40 years, there has been a steady increase in survival rates for blood cancers. Some of those improvements have been dramatic.

Blood cancer research, much of it funded by The Leukemia & Lymphoma Society, has yielded some new and hope-inspiring treatments over the past decade. The most notable is the newly approved drug Gleevec, developed and manufactured by Novartis. Gleevec has been shown to stop the growth of cells responsible for causing chronic myelogenous leukemia (CML) without harming normal cells. Further, it can be taken orally and has limited side effects. Gleevec has resulted in marked improvement in patients with CML. Gleevec is considered to be one of the most successful new treatments for leukemia in decades. A recent study found that over 90 percent of newly diagnosed patients treated with Gleevec as initial therapy had normal blood cell counts one year later. Gleevec is giving hope to thousands of people with CML. It has also created a new paradigm for cancer research.

Research grants from The Leukemia & Lymphoma Society played an important role in the development of Gleevec. With early support and continued funding from the Society, Gleevec's developer, Dr. Brian Druker of the Oregon Health & Science University in Portland, was able to continue his groundbreaking research.

For twelve years, Dr. Druker has searched for key pieces of the puzzle that will lead to cures for blood cancers. One of those keys is Gleevec. In 2002, Dr. Druker continued his fight against blood cancers on a different front, joining Team In Training as an athlete. His goal was to raise awareness about the need for additional money for blood cancer research. On June 2, 2002, he completed the Suzuki Rock 'n' Roll Marathon in San Diego as a proud Team In Training athlete.

 **Connect with your inspiration daily**

Even with the treatment advances and climbing survival rates, blood cancer statistics are sobering. The reality is that these statistics are not just numbers, they're people—children and adults who are struggling to beat their diseases. Each of these people has friends and family members who are struggling with them. It is the personal connection that Team In Training athletes make with blood cancer patients and their families and friends that's often most inspiring.

Each Team In Training athlete is matched with an **honored patient.** Honored patients are usually local individuals, often young people, who are battling a blood cancer. It is in this person's honor that you train for and compete in your endurance race.

When you commit to participating in Team In Training, you receive a hospital I.D. bracelet with the name of your honored patient on it. I can personally tell you that putting that bracelet on for the first time is an awesome experience. You feel a sense of pride and responsibility take hold. When this happens, the Team In Training program has begun to work its magic. Wearing the hospital bracelet reminds you from moment to moment that you're committed to a cause that's much larger than you. The bracelet also serves as a constant reminder of the struggles your honored patient is enduring.

During their training, many athletes have the opportunity to meet and get to know their honored patient. This opportunity is the highlight of the program for many athletes. Honored patients put a face to the diseases you are raising money to fight. Learning about your honored patient's struggles serves as a powerful motivator during your training. While 26.2 miles seems like a long distance to run or 100 miles seems a long distance to cycle, these challenges are dwarfed by the daily struggles of cancer patients fighting their diseases.

The following quote seen on the back of a Team In Training athlete's t-shirt sums it up best:

**"You think training for a marathon is difficult? Try chemotherapy."**

Team In Training's honored patients inspire their athletes to train harder, raise more money, and stay committed longer than any other aspect of the program. Knowing that the money you are raising will help find a cure for your honored patient's disease is often the program's greatest reward.

 **Share your inspiration with others**

In many instances, the inspiration shared between honored patients and their athlete participants is reciprocal. Athletes inspire their honored patients with their commitment to the cause and by their willingness to help complete strangers in their struggle to find a cure for their diseases. The inspiration has gone further in some cases. With increasing frequency honored patients are becoming athletes themselves, when their diseases go into remission. Many are motivated to do so as a result of their experience as an honored patient. Beyond honored patients, it's not uncommon to hear from participants who were inspired to join the program after receiving a fundraising letter from a friend.

In Part Two you'll hear some incredible stories of honored patients turned athletes. Their determination and resolve will amaze you.

Learning about the blood cancers you are working to help cure provides powerful inspiration. Meeting and getting to know the people and families these diseases are attacking further strengthens your resolve. When you join Team In Training, you find and sustain the inspiration you need to exceed your training and fundraising goals.

The inspiration built into Team In Training through education and honored patients is the perfect example of the kind of compelling inspiration you might identify as part of a GAIN Plan.

Looking again at our sample goal of running the 2004 Suzuki Rock 'n' Roll Marathon, here's how the Inspiration portion of your GAIN Plan might look:

# Sample Step 3 GA*I*N Plan Form

*I*NSPIRATION: Identify your compelling Inspiration.

**My true inspiration for reaching this goal is:**

*To improve my health, fulfill an athletic dream, honor someone who is fighting a disease, and raise money to cure blood cancers.*

**Then ask yourself:**

- Have I identified my true inspiration for working towards this goal? *Yes.*

- Can I clearly picture my inspiration for reaching this goal?

I see . . . *the face of my honored patient. I have learned about the deadly blood cancers I'm helping to fight. I can see the graphs that show improvements in cure rates, which are a direct result of fundraising efforts like mine.*

**What will be my tangible connection to my inspiration?**

*My Team In Training hospital bracelet and the photo I have of my honored patient are my tangible connections to my inspiration.*

**How motivated am I by the inspiration I have identified?**
Circle One Number

    **5** = Extremely motivated    ④= Very motivated    **3** = Motivated
        **2** = Somewhat motivated    **1** = Not very motivated

If your answer is less than 3, reconsider setting this goal.

If your answer is 3 or higher, go for it!

# Build Strong Networks of Support

*It's what you know, who you know, and who they know.*

I t's nearly impossible to reach any truly challenging goal without help from others. Think about some of humankind's greatest achievements. While Neil Armstrong gets the credit for being the first person to walk on the moon, it took the dedication and hard work of hundreds of people to get him there. Though Lance Armstrong, a cancer survivor himself, has won the Tour de France bicycle race four times, he admits that he couldn't have done it without his U.S. Postal Team teammates protecting him in the peloton, "pulling" him up mountains, and giving him race information in his earpiece.

Look closely at any successful person and you will find that they had help getting where they are. This is true, without exception, of every senior executive I've worked with from America's most respected companies. In my leadership development courses and in one-on-one coaching sessions, they all tell me the same thing: they received help from some key people along the way to achieving their goals. They had mentors, friends, colleagues, and even strangers who taught, encouraged, supported, and believed in them. For every Olympic gold medalist there were coaches, family members, friends, teammates, and many others who contributed to their success. This is true not only for astronauts, bike racers, corporate executives, and Olympians; it's true for us all. We need strong networks of support to reach our challenging goals.

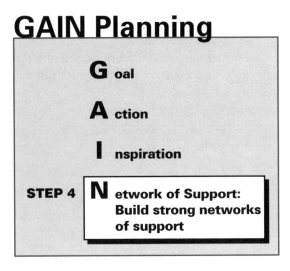

Without them it's impossible to achieve our full potential.

Think about your own proudest achievements. Whose help did you have to reach them? Most likely you had lots of help. As you work towards realizing your future dreams, you will need the assistance of many people. While it would be wonderful if these people magically appeared, it usually doesn't work that way. As the pursuer of your dreams, it's your responsibility to seek out the help you need.

You've probably heard the old adage, "It's not what you know, it's who you know." We usually hear it in reference to someone who has achieved something we feel they didn't deserve, just because they knew the right people. Unfortunately, this negative interpretation misses the key point that who you know, and who you go out and meet, are critically important to reaching your goals. I believe it's truer to say,

*It's what you know, who you know, and who they know.*

Of course your basic knowledge is important, but equally important is the help you enlist from other people to reach your goals. The combination of the two is far more powerful than just knowledge or the right connections are alone.

As soon as you set a challenging goal, start thinking about whose help you'll need to reach it. This support is too important to leave to chance. You'll want to actively seek out and cultivate it. The people you identify will comprise your network of support. They'll provide you with the information, encouragement, connections, and support that will help you get across the finish line of your goal.

A strong network of support includes people who are committed to helping you succeed—people whom you can count on to stick with you over the long haul.

The more difficult your goals, the more important your networks of support become. Here are some things to consider when thinking about whom to include in your networks of support:

- What do I need to learn and who can teach it to me?
- What resources do I need and who can provide them?
- What information do I need and who can supply it?
- Who can best help to keep me motivated?
- Do I know anyone who has accomplished a similar goal?
- Do I know anyone who is currently working towards a similar goal?
- Who can provide me with the feedback I need to measure my progress towards my goal?

# Roles Played by Your Supporters

As you consider these questions, it becomes clear that the people in your networks of support play a number of different roles. They serve as your cheerleaders, coaches, teachers, and mentors. Below are just some of the roles they'll play. Under each role description there's room for you to write the names of one or two people in your life who currently or potentially could play these roles. The same people often can play many different roles for you.

### Cheerleaders

We all need people to cheer us on and encourage us as we put in the sweat and effort required to meet our challenging goals. Make sure you have people in your networks of support who will be your cheerleaders.

My Cheerleaders: _____

_____

### Coaches and Teachers

Some of your goals will require you to learn new skills or sharpen existing ones. Your coaches and teachers assist you in developing the skills you need.

My Coaches and Teachers: _____

_____

## Mentors

Mentors are people you trust and respect. Often, they're people who have achieved things similar to what you are working towards. You can rely on them for sound advice. Mentors are not always easy to find. Don't be afraid to ask for help from people you respect. You may be surprised how flattered they are by your request.

My Mentors: _____

_____

## Confidants

Working towards your dreams is both exciting and frightening. Your confidants are the people you share your excitement, fear, frustration, and joy with as you journey towards your goals. Make sure you have some people in your networks of support who are good listeners.

My Confidants: _____

_____

## Information Providers

Will your goal require specific information you don't currently have? If so, who can provide that information? You will want to include people in your networks of support who can provide you with the information you need.

My Information Providers: _____

_____

## Networkers

Your networkers are the individuals who connect you to the people who can facilitate your success. Select people who have wide personal and professional networks. Also, make sure they'll be willing to open their address books for you.

My Networkers: _____

_____

## Feedback Givers

As you labor towards your goals, it can be difficult to accurately judge your progress. You may feel like you've covered only a mile when in reality you've covered 10. Unfortunately, the opposite can also be true. Because of this, you must rely on people you trust to give you honest feedback on how you're doing. Are you moving in the right direction? Are you making progress? Are there ways you could be more efficient? Accurate and honest feedback is critical to success. You must include people in your networks of support whom you can trust to give it to you.

**My Feedback Givers:** _____

## Accountability Holders

Despite our best intentions, we all get off track from time to time. We stray from our diets, skip workouts, cut classes, or otherwise short-circuit our progress towards our goals. We need people to hold us accountable when this happens. Our accountability holders do just that. They help us stay on track, and when we stray they round us up and get us moving in the right direction again.

**My Accountability Holders:** _____

All of these roles are important. Depending on the nature of your goal, some will be more critical than others. For example, if your goal is to learn to fly an airplane and you know nothing about flying, you will rely heavily on people who can serve as coaches and teachers. On the other hand, if your goal is to meet Mr. or Miss Right, you may need more cheerleaders, confidants, and networkers to help you.

A great example of the need for accountability holders is around diet and exercise goals. You may recall a very public example of this from Oprah Winfrey's life. She had yo-yoed up and down in her weight for years. But when she started working with her personal trainer, Bob Greene, she began to keep her weight off. Ultimately, she ran a full marathon. What was the difference? Besides his training regimen, Bob Greene helped Oprah hold herself accountable. He would meet with her five to six mornings a week, at 5:00 A.M., for her daily run. And how about Oprah's diet? She had help from her personal chef, Rosie Daley. Both Bob and Rosie served to help keep Oprah accountable to her diet and exercise goals.

You don't need a different person to fill each of the identified roles. It's entirely possible that individuals in your network of support will play multiple roles. For example, your teachers and coaches may also hold you accountable and serve as your confidants.

**When building your networks of support, be sure to select people who have both the ability and the willingness to help you succeed.**

As you begin to create GAIN Plans for your goals, it's a good idea to have a pool of potential people to draw on for your networks of support.

**Think about the people in your life whom you trust and respect.** Here is a partial list of people to consider:

- Friends
- Family
- Coworkers (past and present)
- Clients (past and present)
- Teachers (past and present)
- Coaches
- Neighbors
- Professionals whose services you use: lawyers, doctors, accountants
- People who've successfully reached similar goals
- People who are currently working towards similar goals

**From the people who come to mind, choose 10 to potentially include in your networks of support. Indicate what roles they might play.**

| Name | Roles |
|------|-------|
| 1. | |
| 2. | |
| 3. | |
| 4. | |
| 5. | |
| 6. | |
| 7. | |
| 8. | |
| 9. | |
| 10. | |

## Ask for the Help You Need

The people you've identified can only help you if you ask them specifically for what you need. It's much easier to do this once you've identified the other elements of your GAIN Plan. When you know your specific goals, have created solid action plans, and are clear about your inspirations, you can ask for the specific help you need. This is much easier for others to commit to than a general query for help.

For some reason, many people consider asking for help a sign of weakness. I believe the opposite is true. It takes strength and courage to admit you need help and to ask for it. Contrary to what you might expect, the most successful people are often the most willing to ask for help. They know that the likelihood of reaching their challenging goals increases exponentially when they seek help from key people.

In addition to the people you know personally, don't be afraid to ask for help from people you don't know. Some of your more challenging goals will require the help of people you don't know. You may be surprised to find how willing other successful people are to help you, even if they don't know you. The fact is that the same principles you're learning here apply to them. Once upon a time, they also needed help from others to become successful. So helping you reach your goals is a great way for them to return the favor. Seeking their help also validates their success and gives them an opportunity to share what they've learned.

If your request for help is turned down, find someone else who can help and ask them. If they turn you down, keep asking until you find someone who's willing to help.

## Share Your GAIN Plans with Your Supporters

Once you have gained a commitment from others to support you in the pursuit of a goal, share the other elements of your GAIN Plan for that goal with them. It's important that they're connected to your inspiration, know your action plans, understand the obstacles you may face, and are clear about how specific and challenging your goal is in your eyes. Ask for their help and advice in refining your plan. This serves two purposes: you get help creating a winning GAIN Plan and they have an increased stake and sense of ownership in your success.

Beyond the specific people you identify for your networks of support, share your goals with everyone you know. The more people who know what you are working on, the better. You will find that when you share your goals you get assistance, information, and help from people you might never have considered asking.

# The Law of Reciprocity

Often, the quickest route to reaching your goals is to help others reach theirs. If you believe in karma, the more you help others the more you'll get back in return. That is the *law of reciprocity* in GAIN Planning. Bob Greene and Rosie Daley, Oprah's personal trainer and personal chef discussed earlier in this section, are great examples of this principle in action. Bob and Rosie now have fame and wealth beyond what they probably ever imagined. Both have written best-selling books and have been on television shows across the country all because they helped Oprah reach her goals.

As you create GAIN Plans to reach your important goals, consider how you might integrate the law of reciprocity into your plans. Are there ways you can tie your goals to the goals of others in a positive way? What do you have to offer in exchange for help from key people you want in your networks of support? How can reaching your goals create value for someone else?

This book is a perfect example of this win/win philosophy in action. In 1998, after completing the Suzuki Rock 'n' Roll Marathon in San Diego with Team In Training, I had an idea. I thought I could combine my expertise in helping people reach their goals with Team In Training's success story to create an insightful and enjoyable book. For this to work, though, I needed the support and cooperation of The Leukemia & Lymphoma Society.

I knew a few people at my local chapter, but no one at the national level. I asked my contacts to put me in touch with the right people at the Society's Home Office. After a few telephone conversations, I offered to fly from my home in San Diego, CA to the Society's Home Office in White Plains, NY, for a face-to-face meeting. I flew out for one day and met with two vice presidents. During our meeting, I showed them how this book could be a true win/win. The Leukemia & Lymphoma Society gains valuable publicity, a percentage of the proceeds (as a charitable donation), and the opportunity to have their mission proliferated. I get the opportunity to tell Team In Training's inspiring success story and use it as an example of the principles I teach in action. As you can see, they agreed, and together we've created a true win/win.

# Quick Tips

## for Building Strong Networks of Support

- Challenging goals require help
- Determine what help you will need and who can best provide it
- Determine how you will get feedback on your progress
- Ask for the assistance you need
- Share your plans with your supporters
- Be willing to help others

When you begin to think about how you can connect your goals to the goals of others, you make the shift to a win/win paradigm. Once you've done this, you begin to see lots of innovative and exciting ways to get what you want in life.

You'll notice two interesting things start to happen when you begin building strong networks of support. First, they quickly become reciprocal. The people in your networks will begin to seek out your help in reaching their goals. You start becoming a resource to others. This is both exciting and rewarding. It gives you the chance to help others get what they want as well. The second thing is that the people in your networks of support become your biggest fans. They often encourage you to reach for bigger dreams and goals than you previously considered.

Once you've identified the people for your network of support for a specific goal, share the other elements of your GAIN Plan for that goal with them. Seek their feedback and make any adjustments that seem appropriate.

*The fourth step in developing winning GAIN Plans is to build strong networks of support.*

## Your GAIN Planning Tools

Think back to the goal you identified on page 22 one last time. What help will you need to reach this goal? What roles are most important for your supporters to fill? Who can best fill those roles? After considering these questions, complete the Network of Support portion of your GAIN Plan on the following page:

# Step 4 GAI*N* Plan Form

*N*ETWORK OF SUPPORT: Build a strong network of support.

## List a minimum of two people who will comprise my network of support. Indicate how they will help me.

*Ensure that these people have the necessary knowledge and skills and are willing to help me!*

| Name: | How they will help me: |
|---|---|

1. _____

   _____

2. _____

   _____

3. _____

   _____

4. _____

   _____

## With at least one member of my network of support I have:

❑ Reviewed the specificity and challenge of my goal.

❑ Reviewed my action plan and shared my potential obstacles and strategies for overcoming them.

❑ Shared my true inspiration for working towards this goal.

### *GAIN Plan Summary*

Congratulations! You've completed the final step of the GAIN Plan for the goal that you identified at the beginning of this book. Now you're ready to complete the summary "My GAIN Plan" form on the next page. For the action plan, just summarize the main actions you will take and attach the complete form to the summary page. Once you've completed the form, photocopy it and post it where you will see it every day.

**For your review in completing your "My GAIN Plan" Form refer to the following pages.**

| | |
|---|---|
| Goal Statement | Page 22 |
| Action Plan | Page 35 |
| Inspiration | Page 50 |
| Network of Support | Page 67 |

# Apply What You've Learned

At this point in the book you have learned all the fundamentals you will need to develop powerful GAIN Plans. If you took the time to complete your first GAIN Plan as you were reading Part One, you're already well on your way to using the GAIN Planning process to reach your goals. If you skipped the *Tools* sections, it's still not too late to start applying what you've learned. Either way, Part Three has all of the information and forms you'll need to create GAIN Plans for all your individual and team goals. I encourage you to use these resources, as well as the ones you will find online, as part of *Inspiration to Perspiration's* companion website at *www.goalsuccess.com*.

# My GAIN Plan

**G**oal

_____

_____

_____

**A**ction Plan (Summary Statement)

_____

_____

_____

**I**nspiration

_____

_____

_____

**N**etwork of Support

1. _____

2. _____

3. _____

4. _____

❑ My completed Action Plan is attached.

❑ I have shared my GAIN Plan with my network of support.

# Step 4 in Action

## GO TEAM

*It is literally true that you can succeed best and quickest by helping others to succeed.*

Napoleon Hill

Networks of support abound for Team In Training participants; from your teammates whom you train with for four to five months, to your honored patients, coaches, family members and everyone who donates money to the cause in support of your efforts.

Personally, one of the most fulfilling aspects of Team In Training was the connections I made with my teammates. I found that I could get to know a person quite well spending three hours running with them with nothing else to do but talk. In fact, I've even heard of one confirmed marriage between two Team In Training athletes!

**Challenging goals require help**

Team In Training athletes find that their teammates serve as key members of their network of support. They fill important roles such as cheerleaders, confidants, and accountability holders. They best understand the challenges and victories you are experiencing as a developing athlete. They know the commitment your participation requires and they can lend the emotional support you need to persevere. They also make the experience fun. The energy created by the team of people working towards similar goals is extremely exciting and rewarding.

Another important member of your network of support as a Team In Training athlete is your mentor. All athletes are assigned a mentor when they enter the program. The mentors are past Team In Training participants who were successful with their own training and fundraising. They volunteer their time to ensure that future Team In Training participants have as rewarding an experience as they did.

**TIP** ▶ **Determine what help you will need and who can best provide it**

Team In Training mentors help participants meet their training and fundraising goals by conveying information, answering questions, making suggestions, and serving as coaches and teachers. The mentor aspect of Team In Training ensures that each athlete has at least one person in their network of support with the experience and commitment necessary to help them succeed.

Mentor support is not only emotional but physical as well. As the weekend team training runs and rides increase in distance, the importance of water, food, and first-aid stations mounts. Mentors and other volunteers set up and work these stations. They supply the runners and cyclists with water, protein bars, Vaseline (to prevent chafing), and other needs. More importantly, they provide encouragement as the athletes swim, ride, walk, and run farther than ever before. By providing for these basic physical and emotional needs, these mentors and volunteers support the athletes in their quest to reach their goals.

**Ask for the assistance you need**

The fundraising aspect of Team In Training is a great example of the need to ask for help from others. Many athletes send out 50 or more fundraising letters asking for donations in support of the fight to cure blood cancers. Most find the response to their letters to be excellent. An added benefit of asking for this help is that when the letters with donations begin to arrive, your accountability for following through with your goal goes up—*way* up.

As your participation in the program continues, you find that your commitment to success increases with each team run, walk, bike, or swim. Every contact you have with your honored patient encourages you to redouble your efforts. Sending out your fundraising letters greatly expands your network of support. People know the goals you are working towards and go out of their way to support you. Each fundraising check you receive with an accompanying note of encouragement strengthens your commitment. Friends and family continually ask about your training, which is a huge motivator to get out and do it.

When you finally get to your race event you find that your network of support is larger than you ever imagined. The pre-race pasta party is a long-standing Team In Training tradition. The night before your race you gather with participants who have trained together and traveled from all over the country to the race. You enjoy a hearty carbo-loaded pasta dinner and hear speakers including honored patients, family members, volunteers, athletes, and record-setting fundraisers.

It's not uncommon to find yourself at a pre-race pasta party with more than 1,500 other athletes. It's awesome to sit among these teammates, who have faced the same challenges and rewards of training as you. It makes you appreciate that you're part of something monumental. You are making a difference. You've already won.

 **Be willing to help others**

For Team In Training athletes, race day is often the pinnacle of their experience. Adorned in their purple Team In Training race jerseys, they travel the race course to the sound of hundreds chanting "GO TEAM!" Friends, family, coaches, mentors, volunteers, and strangers alike offer support and encouragement. They wave and shout things like, "Looking good," "You're doing great," and "You go girl." Many athletes have a photo of their honored patient pinned to them. Others have the person's name inscribed on the back of their jersey. For others, the familiar hospital I.D. bracelets connect them in spirit to the cancer patient they are honoring.

The support you receive as a Team In Training athlete on race day is overwhelming. It gives you energy when you're lagging and propels you towards the finish line. It's the perfect example of the power of a strong network of support.

You also find yourself compelled to reciprocate the encouragement and support you're receiving. It's a common sight to see hoards of Team In Training athletes clumped together during a race. They share support, encouragement, and laughter, along with water and the occasional energy bar.

The networks of support you build with fellow athletes, as well as mentors, family, friends, donors, and strangers as a Team In Training participant are as strong as they get. It's exactly the kind of network of support you'd want to build as part of any GAIN Plan.

Looking one last time at our sample goal of running the 2004 Suzuki Rock 'n' Roll Marathon in San Diego, here's how the Network of Support portion of your GAIN Plan might look:

# Step 4 GAI*N* Plan Form

*N*ETWORK OF SUPPORT: Build a strong network of support.

**List a minimum of two people who will comprise my network of support. Indicate how they will help me.**

*Ensure that these people have the necessary knowledge and skills and are willing to help me!*

| Name: | How they will help me: |
|---|---|
| 1. My TNT Mentor | By communicating important information, encouraging me, and helping me stay on track. |
| 2. My TNT Coach | By providing me with training schedules and advice on nutrition, injury prevention, and other related topics. |
| 3. My teammates | By running with me on our long group runs, by sharing what they've learned, and by listening to my struggles. |
| 4. My family | By supporting me with their love, encouragement, and willingness to sacrifice time with me while I train. |

**With at least one member of my network of support I have:**

☑ Reviewed the specificity and challenge of my goal.

☑ Reviewed my action plan and shared my potential obstacles and strategies for overcoming them.

☑ Shared my true inspiration for working towards this goal.

# Race Day

For Shari and me, marathon race day was one of the most rewarding experiences of our lives. All our preparation and training came together for an awesome race. As we passed each mile-marker, I thought about the journey that had brought us to the race. From a postcard pulled from the garbage to that first informational meeting when we were so impacted by the posters of cancer patients and survivors. Our network of support was out in force on marathon day. We had friends and family meet us at miles 12, 16, 22, and 26.2. A good friend even woke at 3:30 A.M. to be a volunteer at the mile 16 water station, just to have the chance to cheer us on for 30 seconds. Each supporter we passed helped to refuel us emotionally and physically.

As we rounded the final corner of the race course and saw the arch of balloons in the distance over the finish line, a chill ran down my spine. Our race was almost run. While we certainly weren't going to win, we were winners. As we ran the last .2 miles, I found myself overwhelmed with emotion. The excitement of finishing the race with Shari was mixed with gratitude for Team In Training's role in getting us there, and sadness at the thought of the thousands of patients for whom the outcome of their race is not yet known. As Shari and I approached the finish line, we clasped hands and crossed with our arms high in the air. We'd done it! We were winners!

In Part Two you'll hear from some amazing individuals. Their stories are sure to inspire you to reach for your dreams. I know you will find the inspiration you need to continue your journey to achieving your goals.

# PART TWO

## Inspiration and Perspiration

*Inspiring True Stories
from Team In Training*

*As long as we have hope, we have direction, the energy to move
and the map to move by. We have a hundred different alternatives,
and a thousand paths and an infinity of dreams. Hopeful, we are
halfway to where we want to go; hopeless, we are lost forever.*

Leo Buscaglia

# Cancer Free in 2003

## My Journey to Overcome, Conquer, and Cross the Finish Lines

*Keep going. Keep moving. You'll never know how far you can go if you stop now.*

Running a marathon was never a goal I'd considered. Basketball and tennis were more my style. I would only run the necessary lengths to cover those courts. That changed in the fall of 1997.

My grandmother was an elite marathoner who didn't start running until late in life. She ran the Boston Marathon and ran the St. George Marathon held in St. George, Utah, 10 times, usually winning her age category or placing in the top three. Then, after running at St. George one last time in 1996, she was diagnosed with uterine cancer. She'd always been healthy and as strong as Hercules, so I was shocked at how fast the cancer overpowered her. At her bedside, I promised to run a marathon in her honor.

I had no idea how I would run 26.2 miles, but I laced up my running shoes and took off. Shortly after beginning, my left knee swelled up and I was exhausted. I thought it was normal and that I was just out of shape, but my knee remained swollen. The doctor said it was most likely from the running so I decreased my runs, but the swelling did not decrease. In fact, it got worse. A short time later, I woke up with pain in my left side and a swollen neck. I went for tests to determine what was wrong. Just six months after my grandma died of cancer, I was diagnosed with non-Hodgkin lymphoma stage 111S (involving spleen). I had two tumors in my neck, one in my knee, and my spleen was enlarged.

At this point my prognosis was favorable; with radiation and chemotherapy, I should be well within nine months. Five months later, I was in remission. I thought the battle was over and that I could resume my normal life, so I began my senior year of college at Brigham Young University. But a month into school I was extremely tired again. I had night sweats and I couldn't sleep. I forced myself to classes, but my next check-up confirmed my fears—the cancer was back. I spent six months going through a more gentle form of treatment called immunotherapy. I fought back the nausea and weakness, stayed in classes, and was able to work 20 hours a week as well.

When the school year ended I wanted to get back in shape and reclaim my health. I hadn't considered running yet, for I didn't have the energy, but I played some basketball and tennis. I enjoyed the Fourth of July, as I had gone into remission the day before. However, a week later, when I was playing a game of Ultimate Frisbee, I was hit from behind and suffered a broken back. After surgery, lying flat in bed, unable to feel my legs, I wondered if I'd ever walk again. My doctor said I might, but I'd never be able to run. I thought of my grandmother and wondered if I'd ever be able to fulfill my promise to her. I took my first steps with crutches and, after a lot of physical therapy, I made it around the block. As soon as I could walk to my car, I had to begin cancer treatments again. I'd relapsed, and this time I needed aggressive chemotherapy. I had a lymph node removed from my neck and then began chemo again in November, 1999.

That winter was horrible. I couldn't return to school, I lost all my hair and I was beyond tired. I spent all my time indoors throwing up and trying to avoid winter viruses. One day I got a card in the mail from The Leukemia & Lymphoma Society letting me know about their fundraising program called Team In Training. They said they'd train me to run or walk a marathon if I'd raise money for cancer research and patient aid services. Suddenly, the promise I'd made to my grandmother became real again.

I went to the informational meeting and sat in the back, wearing a wig. I was afraid they wouldn't let me do the program if they thought I might die during the training! I committed to fundraise $3,800 and run the Mayor's Midnight Sun Marathon in Anchorage, Alaska, on June 17, 2000. I had five months to prepare. I also had chemotherapy to do and I wasn't supposed to be outdoors because my lungs couldn't handle cold air. My spinal injury caused sheer pain down my back and through my legs. My leg muscles had atrophied because I'd been in bed so long. I WAS A MESS! However, I was also determined and inspired by the pledge I'd made to my grandmother! I did various things to fundraise the money I'd committed to, which included a benefit concert put on by some friends. I attempted to run daily but often felt light-headed and nauseous from the chemotherapy. When June 17 came around, I just wasn't ready. Since I'd raised the money, I went with the team to Alaska. I did a 5-mile event that day and cheered my teammates on for seven hours until every last person came across the finish line. Though I was happy for them, I was disappointed for myself. Dejected, I went home with no intention of lacing up my running shoes again.

I started my last semester of school at Brigham Young University in the fall of 2000 and began my internship coaching tennis at a high school in Provo. I wasn't myself, though. I was worn out and didn't have the energy to keep going. Not only had I given up on running a marathon, I started missing tennis games and practices due to treatments and feeling sick. Then, during the season, we discovered that the chemotherapy and radiation had caused a secondary cancer called myelodysplastic syndrome, a type of bone marrow cancer sometimes called pre-leukemia.

I was told I had one year to live.

It's funny what happens when you get news like that. My eyes opened to the things going on around me. I saw my tennis girls playing and enjoying their youth. It made me want to be young and carefree again. I decided my battle wasn't over.

In March, 2001, I laced up a new pair of running shoes and decided nothing was going to stop me from achieving my goals. I ran along the river, pushing through pain and fatigue, often pulling off to the side to throw up and regain my balance. Eating was difficult and many nights I couldn't sleep because my legs and lower back hurt so badly. But every morning I got out of bed, even though I knew doing so would bring tremendous pain. I could've stayed in bed, but then I'd have missed out on all that life had to offer, and I intended to live every moment to the fullest.

Every day I fought through fears, tears, pain, and frustration. Every day I wanted to quit. There were even times while running that I commanded myself to stop, but I refused to listen. Each time I told myself, **Keep going. Keep moving. You'll never know how far you can go if you stop now.**

That summer I ran two half marathons, which would have satisfied others, but not me. I WAS GOING TO RUN A MARATHON! I kept training with Team In Training and received lots of support from team members, mentors, honored patients, and my coach, Steven Frisby. I kept going like Forrest Gump, except, unlike Forrest, I knew why I was running. I wanted to run the St. George Marathon, the last marathon my grandmother had run. I signed up and started raising funds.

At 4:00 A.M. Saturday, October 6, 2001, the alarm clock went off and I got out of bed and on my knees to say a prayer. At 6:45 A.M. that same morning, the starting gun went off for the St. George Marathon. My good friends, as well as my mother and aunt, were there to cheer me on. I had struggled during shorter races, but not on marathon day, not with my grandmother helping me. The realization of my promise and dream came closer with every step. I just kept going, one step at a time. I saw many who were healthy struggle and quit, ambulances and police cars taking them away. I prayed throughout the race and was refreshed each time I saw my friends and family at water stops. When the finish line was only 100 meters away I started sprinting and began to cry. I was afraid I'd pass out, but I didn't, and I finished in 5 hours and 27 minutes. Overcome by my emotions, I couldn't move forward to the crowds of friends and family waiting to embrace and congratulate me. Then, a sweet smile of victory swept across my face . . . I DID IT!

Many times during my cancer battle I had restless, sleepless nights, cursing at the walls because the pain and fatigue were so great. Other times I opened up scriptures and prayed for strength. One night I came across Isaiah in the Old Testament and read a scripture which has become my favorite to this day:

"But they that wait upon the Lord shall renew their strength; they shall mount up their wings as eagles; they shall run and not be weary; and they shall walk and not faint."

I longed for that day when I would run and not be weary and walk and not faint, but I knew it wouldn't come without patience and determination. I had to wade through illness, pain, fatigue, depression, and feelings of failure before I could accomplish my goal. What a sweet day it was when I **finally** did it. Was that my one and only marathon? No way! I'm addicted and training for my next one! I'm also training to do a century ride and an Olympic distance triathlon with Team In Training. I'm an honored patient, but also a team member. I want to wipe out cancer and accomplish amazing personal feats in the process.

The month following the marathon I had leg surgery and feared my leg would have to be amputated since the cancer had spread to the bone. I then began new treatments that hadn't existed when I first began my cancer battle. The research funded by The Leukemia & Lymphoma Society found a treatment that my body responded to. The treatments were successful, and three days before I carried the Olympic torch for the Salt Lake 2002 Winter Games I was deemed cancer free. I held the torch a little higher on behalf of all those who have bravely fought challenges in their lives and symbolize the Olympic theme, "light the fire within." I did it Grandma! I did it! ■

*Shawna Fisher*

# The Inaugural Team

*Sometimes these things are not entirely altruistic, because we respond aggressively in order to ease our own pain. While on one level we're doing it for ourselves, we have the comfort of knowing what we are doing also has considerable benefit for others.*

U ntil March 21, 1986, my wife Isobel (Izzi) and I had lived a pretty normal life with the same kinds of ups and downs and high points and low points as everyone else. It had been a very positive, reaffirming kind of life. On that fateful day in 1986 we learned that our daughter, Georgia, had leukemia. It was the week before Easter, and Georgia was two years and three months old.

We had two other children at the time, Samantha and James. Several years later, in 1990, we had Mark, our fourth child. We were active with good careers and many interests; we traveled widely and had a diverse group of friends in many countries. We had our challenges, just like anyone else, but even the challenges were mostly good.

I was in my office when I received Izzi's tearful call and I will never forget it. An icy chill went down my spine. I grabbed my coat and ran out.

From there it was a blur of fear, apprehension, and paralyzing frustration. We were used to managing our lives and circumstances, but now we were facing an impossibly scary situation over which we had no control. I still remember so clearly, later that first day, the pediatrician saying, "I don't mean to frighten you, but you must understand that your lives will never be the same." I don't think we really understood what he meant, but he was right, our lives have never been the same.

After dealing with the shock of Georgia's diagnosis and the difficulty of the treatment that followed, we contacted the Leukemia Society of America* to ask if we could help in their fundraising efforts. We wanted Georgia's illness to lead to something positive, hopefully even a cure. Over the next 20 months we helped organize a number of different fundraising events, including a black tie ball and a car raffle. These events were quite successful, but they were hard work and they required us to keep going back to the same community of friends to ask for their financial support. One day, one of our very good friends said, "It sure is expensive to be your friend," and he was right. I began musing on ideas where we could use leverage, the same way we do in business, to reach a wider community of participants and donors.

Late one evening in 1987, after a black tie ball, a bunch of us were relaxing and brainstorming ideas for what else we could do to raise money. It was then that the idea for a different kind of fundraiser slowly began forming.

The ball had been a big success and we were absolutely exhausted. As I sat slumped in my chair, looking down at my stomach, I thought, "God I'm in terrible condition!" I had always been fairly athletic, but a few years earlier I'd had knee surgery, that, in addition to my chaotic schedule, had prevented me from running. My thoughts then drifted to the 1983 New York City Marathon and to a New Zealand friend of mine named Rod Dixon. Rod was a world-class runner and an Olympic medal winner. When Rod won the New York City Marathon in 1983, he, his wife, and their two daughters had stayed with us at our home in Rye, New York. I remember thinking, "I'd love to be able to run a marathon, but there's no way I can because I've got buggered knees."

And then the words came out of my mouth—I suggested we get a group of non-athletes together, train them, and run a marathon together for the cause.

---

*In 2000, the Society changed its name from The Leukemia Society of America to The Leukemia & Lymphoma Society to emphasize its commitment to fighting all blood cancers.

This would have seemed absurd, even to me—I was 40, an ex-rugby player, and badly out of shape—had I not just read an inspiring article in the New York Post. The article was about Bob Wieland, a Vietnam war veteran from California who'd lost both of his legs to a land mine, all the way up to his torso.

He competed in endurance events not in a wheelchair but by propelling himself with two wooden rockers that he wore on his hands. He supported his torso on a small homemade skateboard and propelled himself forward using only his arms. In 1986, it took him four days, two hours, forty-eight minutes, and sixteen seconds to complete the New York City Marathon. In 1987, he improved his time to three days, nine hours, thirty-seven minutes, and forty-five seconds—more than a day faster!

I felt like a wimp. Here I was with four mainly good limbs and just a couple of bad knees. Surely there was some way I could get into shape and run a marathon.

Later that night, I found myself lying in bed amongst a jumble of thoughts. Could we find a group of "former athletes" like me who would love the opportunity to truly transform themselves over a period of 10 months? Could we create some real human interest? Could we get corporate and individual sponsors to participate on a scale that would make it interesting? Could we raise some **really serious** money? Could I get my friend Rod Dixon involved? Rod was a very big name in marathon running, particularly in New York, and he could be our team coach.

I couldn't stop thinking about it, and after a restless night, I hopped out of bed early the next morning and called a buddy of mine, Geoff Andrews, who lived in Los Angeles. Geoff is a couple of years older than I and is also a former rugby player with bad knees. More importantly, Geoff has a huge heart. Geoff answered the telephone in a groggy voice and I spilled out my thoughts in a stream of consciousness. He just listened to me, saying nothing, the way someone who's half-asleep does. Finally, when I paused, he said, "You've got to be crazy!" and hung up the phone. It was only then that I realized I'd forgotten about the three-hour time difference between NY and LA. It was 7:00 A.M. in NY, so I had just called him at 4:00 A.M. LA time. No wonder he'd sounded so sleepy and cranky!

Several hours later, Geoff called back and asked me to repeat my idea. When I finished, he said, "I think you're bloody crazy, but if you do it, I'll do it," and at that moment, I knew we had a team.

So I decided I would pull together a team of people who each knew someone who was battling, or had died from, leukemia. This group of mostly over-forty non-athletes would train together to run the 1988 New York City Marathon.

I would secure a running coach, work with the Leukemia Society, and handle the logistics of the team. In exchange for marathon training, each team member would be expected to raise $5,000, through individual and corporate sponsorships, for the Leukemia Society. The team's fundraising goal would be an ambitious $150,000.

Unsure if I could generate enough interest to get even ten or fifteen people to join the team, I was amazed when 35 people showed up for the initial information meeting. In all, 44 people—36 men and eight women—joined.

On a Sunday afternoon in February, 1988, we got our recruits together for our first team training session. We enlisted the help of our friend Suzie Joyce, an aerobics instructor, to take us through our first workout. It was not a pretty sight. Partway through the session, Norman Berkowitz, our team physician and the same doctor who had diagnosed Georgia, came over to me and said, "Are you serious?" He and Suzie felt that some members of our team were in too poor of physical shape to run a marathon. They suggested that we abandon the exercises and just do some light stretching. We did and, in addition, we had each participant speak with Norman one-on-one. He gave each of them a quick five-minute physical and told some to go and see their own personal physicians to get a proper medical clearance.

From that point on it all began to take shape. We were flying completely blind, at times not knowing what it was we were trying to do, let alone how we were going to do it. Another friend, Bob Greene, who is in the advertising business, came to my home one rainy Sunday afternoon. We sat together discussing the group marathon training concept and trying to decide on a name for the event. "Team In Training" was the name we agreed on. We then sketched out a logo very similar to the one used today. Bob and I designed a small brochure to be used as a mailing piece that would explain what we were doing and list all the members of the team. It included photographs of Rod Dixon, Leonard Marshall (NY Giants), and Gary Carter (NY Mets), all of whom had agreed to lend their names to the event.

My office quickly became "mission control" for Team In Training, and at times it felt like Grand Central Station. Calls were coming in from all over the country and around the world, and at times we were swamped with people asking where they could send their checks. As the momentum began to build, it was truly amazing to see the powerful effect of the "law of large numbers." Forty team members, each spoke with friends, family members and business associates, and these people, in turn, spoke to others, and then they all began sending checks. We eventually had to redirect all of the correspondence to the Westchester Leukemia Society chapter office. Rochelle Kaufman, the executive director there, had to hire an assistant to deal with all the logistics.

The inaugural Team In Training group trained together for six months, with most members running six days a week. The group joined each other as often as possible on weekends for team runs and aerobics workouts.

Finally, the day of the race arrived, and every TNT team member who started the race finished. We held a presentation ceremony and reception after the race at the St. Moritz Hotel on Central Park South. We had raised more than $320,000 for leukemia research. We were elated! We had also collectively lost more than half a ton of weight!

When I look back, I can't quite believe we did it. Logistically, we had no support or infrastructure and staying in close contact with all those people for 10 months was difficult without e-mail.

By early 1989, with the first Team In Training marathon behind us, Izzi and I realized there had hardly been a conversation that had begun or ended in our house without the word leukemia in it. Our involvement had been a mainly positive experience, and it had helped us get through some dark moments, but we realized we had responsibilities to our other two children as well as to Georgia.

Initially we considered just reducing our involvement, but we realized that would be impossible. We recognized that we were both so involved, there could be no halfway. We would have to let go completely. Most importantly, we realized that getting the word leukemia out of our family's lexicon was very important for Georgia's cure.

At the end of 1992, we moved from New York to Maryland and I took a job as president of Campbell & Company. In March 1997, a colleague of mine, Arden Travers, put a brochure on my desk and asked whether I, or the company, would sponsor her for a Team In Training event. It was an event in which participants would compete in the 86-mile Athens-to-Atlanta (A2A) in-line skating race. The race was to take place in October of that year. I said I would happily sponsor her, but only if I could do the race as well.

The following weekend, Arden and I began training with the Washington Team In Training A2A team. A short time later we established a Maryland team to make our training easier. We managed to get a team of eighteen people together to train and skate the A2A, and we've done the race almost every year since then.

Georgia had a very bad prognosis at the time of her initial diagnosis. Her white blood cell count was highly elevated and she was in very bad shape. The only way they could stabilize her was with very aggressive treatments, and this got her into remission quite quickly. Thankfully, she has held her remission from then until now.

The chemotherapy and radiation therapy protocols used fifteen years ago were much heavier and more aggressive than those used today. Consequently, the same treatment protocols that saved Georgia's life also hurt her. Early on, we were told that Georgia would need cranial radiation therapy. This is very serious, especially for such a young person. We had to sign a scary indemnity document at the hospital where she was to have this treatment. It basically said, "We're probably going to damage or kill your child, but if we do, you can't sue us."

On the other hand, they told us that if she didn't have that treatment there was a ninety percent probability that she would develop a brain tumor within three years. They also said that the cranial radiation would cost her a few IQ points. I remember joking that all of our children had IQ points to burn, so Georgia could afford to lose a few.

Unfortunately, it cost her more than a few. Although Georgia has been cancer-free for 16 years, she suffered some brain damage and now has serious learning disabilities. She also has many collateral issues including hormone and growth problems. Georgia is now 18 and life is not easy for her, but I do believe that every cloud has a silver lining. Team In Training is certainly one of them. Another one is the Odyssey school for children with special learning needs. When we moved to Baltimore we could not find a school suitable for Georgia's circumstances, so Izzi helped to start one. It is called the Odyssey School and it has been successful beyond our wildest dreams. Although Georgia is now too old to attend Odyssey, we recently helped finance a new campus for the school that will allow it to accommodate about 160 children.

Sometimes these things are not entirely altruistic because we respond aggressively in order to ease our own pain. While on one level we're doing it for ourselves, we have the comfort of knowing what we are doing also has considerable benefit for others. ∎

*Bruce Cleland*

# Epilogue to The Inaugural Team

After the program's initial success as a volunteer effort, the Team In Training concept was adopted by The Leukemia & Lymphoma Society as a sponsored charity event. Initially, it was limited to only a couple of the Society's 60 Chapters. Each chapter trained one or two teams for a couple of races each year. After the first few years the program began to expand rapidly.

By 1993, five years after its inception, Team In Training had grown to 650 athletes who raised more than $1.2 million. By this time, the program had expanded from one Society chapter to 20. The following year, 1994, saw the program more than triple in size to 1,650 participants and $3.7 million raised. Just one year later, in 1995, the program tripled again in participation to 5,000 participants and almost tripled in funds raised to $9.1 million. By 1995, 57 chapters were participating. From there the program's explosive growth continued. Take a look:

| | |
|---|---|
| 1996 | Marathon walking is added for the first time. This year, 7,000 participants raise $16 million. |
| 1997 | Century cycle events are added. The TNT explosion continues—10,000 participants raise $26.7 million. |
| 1998 | 17,000 participants raise over $40 million. |
| 1999 | This year, 24,000 participants raise $61 million. Triathlon debuts, making TNT a four-sport campaign: Walk, run, cycle, and triathlon. |
| 2000 | Nearly 30,000 participants raise $74 million! TNT is the largest endurance sports training program in existence. |
| 2001 | Over 30,000 participants raise over $78 million! |

What began as a small volunteer effort has grown into one of the most professionally run training and fundraising programs in existence. This happened due to the vision and hard work of numerous people within The Leukemia & Lymphoma Society. Team In Training's current success was made possible by the tireless efforts of the Society's exceptional staff.

Individuals and teams within the Society took the basic Team In Training concept and continually built upon it. Numerous innovative ideas, combined with ever more organized logistical support, helped the program to experience unprecedented growth.

Here are just some of the innovative ideas that have been added over the years to enhance the program:

- A professional coaching staff
- Fundraising support
- Paid travel to desirable race locations
- Formal mentoring
- An honored patient program
- Marathon walking
- Century cycle races
- Triathlon
- Centralized training and fundraising design
- Corporate sponsorships
- Partnerships with race organizers

These innovations and many more, combined with effective marketing strategies, have contributed to the program's growth and popularity.

# From Couch Potato
# to Athlete

*There were times I walked. There were times I felt pain. But there was never a time when I thought I couldn't make it.*

I was a major couch potato. While I accomplished the major things I set out to do in life like go to college, get a job, and become a teacher, these were things I knew I'd do. But run a marathon? I don't think so!

On a January afternoon in 1998 my life changed. David, my husband, was going through the mail and, as usual, he was throwing it out before I had a chance to look through it. As I walked by, a purple and green post-card caught my eye. I grabbed it and saw that it was from a group called Team In Training. They said they could train anyone to run or walk a marathon. When I saw that, I thought, "I'm anyone." Now honestly, had it not been the first week in January I don't know that I would have paid any attention to the card, but I figured, "What's one more New Year's Resolution to break?" I had broken so many before. (Especially those requiring me to get in shape). I showed the card to David and he said he'd join me.

When we went to the informational meeting held at our local Red Cross, I thought, "What have I gotten myself into?" Luckily, there were speakers who had already done the program, one of whom was a former couch potato like me. That did it. I signed up and received an informational packet and bracelet with the name of the honored patient I would be running for, Laura Williams. Her strength would be my inspiration for the next five months of training. I was committed.

When I told my family and friends what I was doing, some of them chuckled. They knew how lazy I was when it came to exercising. They were supportive, but I knew they had their doubts. And why shouldn't they? I had my own doubts. But the more people I told, the more committed I became. I was not going to quit this time.

The first run with TNT was at the beach. When I got there, people were stretching, so I joined in. (Never mind the fact that I had no clue what I was doing.) A TNT coach came over and began explaining the types of stretches we should do and when. Ah, salvation, someone who would help me through. Then we began our three-mile run, the first of many, many runs to come. Before I was halfway through I started breathing heavily and my body started to ache. Again I wondered what I was doing. It was a question I would ask many more times during my training.

That first run was horrible. I learned what years of sitting on the couch had done to my body. At work that Monday I proudly told my boss that I had run three miles. I was so excited! She encouraged me, telling me she knew I'd reach my goal. I began to feel a sense of pride that I still maintain today.

The next step was getting started on fundraising for The Leukemia & Lymphoma Society. I sent cards and asked for donations and I quickly raised the required funds. I was amazed at how many people were willing to help, but I was never too worried about that aspect of the program. My fear was, "Will I make it through the miles and miles of training runs I have ahead of me?"

David and I usually trained together, but I did two runs without him and they stand out as personal milestones for me. One was an eight-mile run I did with the team. During the run I decided to try to keep up with a woman running just ahead of me. I was able to keep up, but I must admit that I was relieved when she started walking! She was my inspiration for that run. And, it was on that run that I became confident that I'd make it through the program.

The second run was twelve miles in the pouring rain. David was out of town and I was warm and snuggly in my bed when the alarm went off at 5:45 A.M. Since the weather was bad, I assumed the team wouldn't train. I decided I'd go, and then when they weren't there, I wouldn't feel guilty about not running. You can imagine my surprise when I saw them. I got out of my car and began to run. I ran, and ran, and ran. And I finished! Another goal completed. Who was I? This was no one I had ever known before. Dare I say I was becoming an athlete?

And this is how it went. Week after week I would accomplish what I set out to do. And week after week I would be surprised to see the person I was becoming. It was overwhelming.

Race weekend arrived. The night before the race, the team gathered for a final meeting. The coach took us through a guided imagery. She told us to visualize ourselves crossing the finish line. As I did, I shed my first tear. I couldn't believe I'd made it this far. Even if I didn't make it across the finish line, I'd made it through the program and I was proud of myself!

It was still dark when I got up on marathon day. I had carefully laid out my clothes so I wouldn't forget anything. David and I drove to the race site, stretched, and got in line. After standing for a few minutes among the 21,000 runners, I looked around. Right behind me was the runner I'd followed on my eight-mile run! She'd inspired me to run eight miles then, and now she'd inspire me to run 26.2! I thought of Laura Williams, my other inspiration, and began to run.

Our family and friends were there, spread out across the course. Whenever we saw them, our pace quickened and we broke into smiles. There were times I walked. There were times I felt pain. But there was never a time when I thought I couldn't make it.

As I write this, my eyes well up with tears. The miles and miles of training for the race, and the 26.2 I did that day, are a part of defining who I am today.

I am no longer a couch potato. I am an athlete.

As I turned the corner to run the last .2 miles, I saw a huge banner that read FINISH. My feet kept running and my face kept smiling. I was in my groove when I heard a voice from the sidelines "Go Shari. You go girl!" I turned around to see my friend Angie standing there with other friends yelling their support. Tears started to run down my face as David grabbed my hand. Together, with our hands raised, we crossed the finish line.

I RAN A MARATHON! ∎

*Shari Jacobson*

# Ten Life Lessons

*Life Lesson number five,* Touch as many lives as you can. *Every time you meet someone new, you leave a little bit of yourself with them. They are affected by you. The more people you meet, the more complete both their and your lives are because of how you have been affected by each other. Think of the possibilities.*

My daughter Kim was looking directly into my eyes when she spoke these words as she delivered her high school graduation speech. They are lesson number five of her ten life lessons. Life lessons that have become my inspiration and the guide for how I live my life.

Sharing Kim's life lessons has become my mission and my way of remembering and honoring her. Whether at a business meeting or a Team In Training pre-race pasta party, I take every opportunity I can to spread her wisdom. I'll share her lessons with you here, but first let me tell you a little about Kim and what led her to write them.

In the spring of 1997, Kim's world was full of possibilities. A sophomore in high school, she was taking driver's education, involved in drama, the YMCA, and heading for Spain with her Spanish Club. But, when she returned from Spain, the course of our lives was permanently altered. Kim was diagnosed with Hodgkin's disease.

While we were shocked by her diagnosis, we were happy to learn that her type of cancer had a very high cure rate. Over the next seven months Kim went through brutal chemotherapy and radiation, which we all believed would successfully bring on a cure.

For the ten months following Kim's treatment, life got back to normal with just occasional visits to the clinic for check-ups. In September of Kim's senior year of high school, we learned that Kim's cancer was back. She endured many more chemotherapy treatments, but this time she became chemo resistant. It became clear to her doctors that she would not survive.

Now imagine being a teenager and getting the news that you have an incurable illness. As Kim's doctors and nurses waited for her reaction, she silently reflected on what the news meant. When she finally spoke, she said, "Will I be able to donate some of my organs?"

We looked at her in awe. Where did this strength come from? How could Kim think of others at a time like this? She was just a teenager.

After that day, we began to understand how she could do this. You see, Kim never forgot she was alive. She never took life for granted. She understood the reality of her disease, but since she felt well, she lived well.

For three years, through her disease and treatment, Kim continued to live with her ever-present "Get out of my way" attitude. She attended school, got her driver's license, joined the National Honors Society, worked as a camp counselor, did cancer fundraising, attended both her junior and senior proms, and much more.

She was a girl who had focus and liked to be in control. A great example was when she joined the prom committee senior year because she wanted her prom to be perfect. And it was.

She wore a beautiful blue gown and looked like Cinderella. On the day of the prom, Kim and a bunch of her pals went to her friend Anna's house to primp. Kim didn't have much primping to do, as she was bald from her chemo treatments, but she still glowed. We parents went along for photo ops in Anna's garden, and then off they went. During the evening, the chaperones voted for the king and queen of the prom. Their selection was based on who was having the best time and partying the hardiest.

Kim was voted queen, much to her surprise. She'd never considered herself to be in the running for such an honor. She was flabbergasted at the ovation, and later, when she told us about it, she beamed.

By March of 2000, it was clear that the cancer was taking its toll. Although Kim stayed as active as possible until May, we knew the end was drawing near. Two days before Kim died, her mother Carol and I, along with her friends Jeremy, Jessica, Jessie, and Hanna, as well as Elizabeth, one of Kim's favorite nurses, planned "The Great Escape."

The idea was to break her out of the hospital on a beautiful summer day! We worked together and positioned oxygen tanks along our escape route, and we arranged for a wheelchair and IV pole for the three different pumps Kim was hooked to.

Jeremy, in his normal outrageous style, wore a trench coat. From outside Kim's door he sang the song from Mission Impossible.

When we were ready, Jeremy did a "John Belushi," jumping with his feet wide apart as he looked both ways down the hall. The coast was clear!

All of a sudden, we appeared in her room. Jeremy guarded the door as we got Kim from the bed to the chair and moved her lines. We told Kim, "We're breaking you out of this place!" She smiled as we worked feverishly to move her.

We brought Kim down the hall, to the elevator, down more halls, and finally outdoors! We spent about 20 minutes outside behind the hospital with her friends—talking, laughing, and simply sharing good, warm feelings.

The next day Kim slept through the morning and I wondered if she'd gone into a coma. Then, in the early afternoon, she woke up and "ate like a horse." She hadn't done that in a long time.

As evening drew near, Kim asked if she could do another great escape. She said, "I want to see the stars." Carol and I got the wheelchair and the I.V. pole, but there weren't enough nurses to help. We reluctantly put Kim back to bed, where she went to sleep.

Kim never woke up the next day, July 24, 2000. She passed away later in the afternoon, surrounded by many of her friends, her favorite teacher from school, her favorite nurses, and her family. We had the CD from Camp Takodah, her favorite place (YMCA camp) playing. While Taps played in the background, Kimberly passed on.

My only regret was that we could not get her outside to see the stars the night before. But I can't help thinking, that maybe, when she went to sleep that final night, her journey to the stars had already begun.

In her typical fashion, since she'd felt so strongly about how her passing should happen, she'd begun planning her funeral, in detail, a full year before she died.

She wanted to have a life celebration and set up a network from our community to throw a party as part of the funeral. She'd been moved by the Columbine, Colorado, massacre and thought the white caskets that people could write on were a great idea. With the dark humor we had grown to appreciate she said, "I'll have plenty of time to read." She suggested that the headstone for her cemetery plot be a bench because her friends might want to sit and visit once in a while, and they do. She even helped write her obituary and insisted that we add the line "Please do not wear black or any color of mourning to the service."

Kim knew what she was doing, and the day of her funeral was beautiful. If you didn't know Kim had died you would have thought it was a wedding. She planned carefully and thoughtfully, because she wanted her friends and family to be okay when she died.

She asked her best friend, Jessica Young, to give her eulogy. Here's a brief excerpt:

> *She now soars above our mountains, a guardian angel in the sky, guiding us all with her spirit. She'll guide Adam (her younger brother) as he flirts with trouble in his high school and college years. She'll give Barry the strength to complete the marathon this winter. She'll remind Carol of the importance of laughter.*
>
> *As for the rest of us, she's given us confidence, strength, and a new perspective on life. Learn from her and listen to her message.*
>
> *Celebrate her life as she soars above us all today.*

I can think of no better introduction to Kim's ten life lessons. Here they are:

**Life Lesson number 10 is *"Deal with life one day at a time."*** Sometimes when life gets crazy we feel like we'll never sort everything out. But if we just deal with everything one day and instance at a time, life just has a way of working through things. It also makes life's circumstances a little less overwhelming.

Life Lesson number 9 is more a word of advice. *"Turn every life experience into a learning experience."* The best way I have found to cope with hard times more easily is to become knowledgeable about what is going on and try to find a meaning to everything that happens. Trust me, there is always one there.

Life Lesson number 8 is *"Always look for the positive."* No matter how bad life can get, there is always a positive to be found. If you focus on the positive aspects of life, the hard times are easier to get through. The power of positive thinking is amazing, and it works.

Life Lesson number 7 is another piece of advice. *"Try to do at least one new thing every day."* Much too often, people get into a routine of doing the same thing every day and their lives become boring. The new thing doesn't have to be big. It can be something really small like taking a different route to work, or trying a new kind of food. Make a wish list for yourself of new stuff you want to try. Some things can be small, and others, big. Plan on completing one of those things each day and by the end of every day your life will be that much more full.

Life Lesson number 6 is *"Be true to yourself."* No matter what happens in your life, if you are true to yourself and confident about who you are, you can overcome anything. Always stick to who you are and don't worry if people are going to accept you or not. If you are confident with yourself, it will show, and the people who really matter will accept you for who you are, not for who you are not.

Life Lesson number 5 is *"Touch as many lives as you can."* Every time you meet someone new you leave a little bit of yourself with them. They are affected by you. The more people you meet, the more complete both their, and your, lives are because of how you have been affected by each other. Think of the possibilities.

Life Lesson number 4 is *"Enjoy the little things."* Although the big accomplishments in life are important, sometimes it's the little things in life that are more enjoyable. The conversations with your best friend in the middle of the night, or a quiet moment somewhere peaceful where you were just able to think, can add up to be much more important and memorable than any big thing.

**Life Lesson number 3 is** *"Don't sweat the small stuff."* Many times in life, people begin getting concerned with petty things. What people forget is that, in the long run, it doesn't matter what "he said" or what "she did." It's not worth your time to get worked up about anything small or petty.

**Life Lesson number 2 is** *"Hold on to your friends."* No matter what happens in your life, good or bad, your friends will be there for you. Whether it is a pat on the back or a shoulder to cry on that you need, your friends are there for you always.

**And the number 1 Life Lesson is** *"Make every day count."* Life is short and we never know how long we are going to have. We must live life to the fullest EVERY DAY. Everything we do should have a greater purpose. We should never throw any opportunities away.

Our lives will continue to be impacted by our friendships, generosity, compassion, and spirit. As each of us works each day to be the person we want to be, remember my favorite quote from the Broadway play *Rent*: "No day but today."

Thank you for helping me keep Kim's spirit alive by reading and sharing her message. And to those of you involved in Team In Training I say this: **WE WILL WIN THIS BATTLE AGAINST CANCER!** Your legs, hearts, and spirits will move us towards a cure! ∎

*Barry Costa*

# Last But Not Forgotten

*I can't capture in words how I feel, but I can say that I'm proud to be a part of something so extraordinary. It will always have a place in my heart.*

Ironman Canada took place on Sunday, August 26, 2001, from 7:00 A.M. to midnight in a little town called Penticton (a five-hour drive east from Vancouver). The race consisted of a 2.4-mile swim, 112-mile bike, and 26.2-mile run. I trained for 10 months with 54 Team In Training teammates. This is my story, as best I can recall.

3:45 A.M.: Wake up, eat breakfast with teammates. Feel relaxed, calm, and happy, but notice congested head, dull headache, and sore throat. Allergies? Can't be dehydrated. I've drunk enough water. Must have coffee. What's my name again?

6:30 A.M.: Walk down to beach surrounding Lake Okanagan. Still dazed but coffee kicking in. There are 1,990 athletes in wetsuits and blue/green caps. Can't see them all without turning my head. It's the largest mass-start swim in Ironman history. Panic. Why am I spending my energy this way? Practice Coach Kate's breathing, like I'm cooling off soup.

7:00 A.M.: BOOM! The cannon goes off, and the lake turns into a washing machine on spin cycle. I let the insane swimmers go first. They'll finish in 45 minutes—twice my pace. I'm in. First mile's okay, but breathing's erratic and head feels congested. Notice sore throat. Ignore. Denial about being sick is a beautiful thing. Goggles fog up so I draft off guy in front of me. Smile to scuba diver (he checks for anything illegal like fins or hand paddles). He smiles back, gives me thumbs up—cool!

8:53 A.M.: I change from the swim to the bike in 5:55 minutes! Not sure how. Ride out of transition area; crowd roars! I feel like Lance Armstrong!

11:00 A.M.: Gorgeous scenery with hills like Hawaii, cliffs like Half Dome in Yosemite, lakes like Lake Tahoe, and dry valleys like Arizona. Love being an Iron Tourist, but just want shade to get a break from the ninety-degree temps. Every 15 minutes I eat a quarter Cliff Bar and drink water or Gatorade. At mile 60 I run out of food as planned. But the Special Needs bag area isn't until mile 75. Eat bananas at water stops, take one, eat another and another. Stomach loves bananas; brain knows I'm human, not monkey.

3:30 P.M.: Richter Pass, mile 70. Not as hard as the Bay Area hills. Tell that to my stomach. Get off to walk, feel like getting sick. Why did I eat so many bananas? Motorcycle officials (man and woman on one bike) stop, give me their ice-cold water bottle, tell me to keep going no matter what. I get sick. Stay away from bananas! Dehydrated, I force fluids in small sips. Thank God for the aerobar water bottle. Ouch, bug dies on arm! At least it's not on my face.

4:30 P.M.: Last big climb, Yellow Lake, mile 90. Sick of heat and climbing. On top of hill a woman rides past (Lynee) and says, "We're going to make the cutoff! We're doing it!" Coach Wayne (a saint) is at the top. "Go get 'em girl! Fly down this hill like you've never flown! Dig deep, lay into it, Alison!" I shout, "Can I make the cutoff?" He says, "Push it hard, like never before!" I hit a personal record—43.3 mph! Happy, Wayne?

5:20 P.M.: Two miles before the bike/run cutoff at 5:30, but there's traffic. The couple on the motorcycle yell, "Follow us, you WILL make it, go as fast as you can, you WILL do this!" They speed into the intersection and stop the cars! I pump my bike as fast as I can (25 mph on the flats). My heart beats like a hummingbird. I follow the motorcycle. People look at me like I'm the president or something. I make the cutoff by two minutes! It's insane!

5:28 P.M.: In the transition tent I sit down next to Lynee, who says, "See, I told you we'd make it!" A volunteer helps me put on sunscreen, race belt (holds the bib #), run shorts, dry socks, shoes, and IronTeam cap. Take deep breaths to slow breathing from bike sprint. Heart races from excitement and adrenaline.

5:45 P.M.: I see my boyfriend Todd bike by. I call out. He doesn't look and is serious and sad. He missed the cutoff by 15 minutes. With his recent foot injury, he must be in a lot of pain. It's bittersweet (we usually run together). Banana attack! Make it to the bathroom just in time. Stomach's better, but head's worse and breathing's shallow. Keep moving.

7:00 P.M.: "Man you're hard to catch!" It's Lynee. She says Coach Wayne sounds like her husband (also in the race). Every time an Iron Teammate passes she's impressed with how we support each other. She wishes there was a team in her hometown.

9:00 P.M.: Coach Wayne appears on his mountain bike and stays with us from mile 10 through mile 26. As it gets dark, there are no streetlights (just the lake, moon, and crickets). We scan the road to make it easier to see, like he taught us. Hard to figure out my pace. Pissed at the world because my body's shutting down and I have a cutoff time to make. It's not pretty.

10:00 P.M.: Coach Wayne won't go away. As much as I love him and the IronTeam I want to stop. Feel bad he's out so late (I'm the last teammate on the course) and say, "You could be in bed." He says, "I'm exactly where I want to be. Right here. Right now."

11:15 P.M.: I see lights! Where's Lynee? Wayne says, "Catch her, run to her!" She's just one minute ahead, but I can't catch up. My legs ache like I have the flu and I'm angry that I'll miss the cutoff. I want to sleep. It's the couple on the motorcycle again, "Way to go Alison! You're doing it! You're an Ironman!"

11:40 P.M.: Todd's running at my side!? Waited for six hours!? Happy, but can't show it. Must finish. See Coach Wayne. "Where's finish?" So many emotions, so little control. So tired.

11:56 P.M.: The race announcer, "Louie, you're an Ironman!" My heart sinks with emotion! Louie's an inspiration. His life's a race against the clock and the Ironman is his dream, and he did it! It's amazing to hear his name! Way to go Louie!

12:00 A.M.: I'm pissed. Missed the cutoff; can't see the turnout point. Todd still with me. Coach Kate appears. "I'm a mess Kate; look at me!" She laughs, "You can't be that much of a mess if you KNOW you're a mess." I'm cranky. "I can't understand anything profound; can't you see I'm a mess?" She laughs. I don't know why.

12:08 A.M.: Coach Kate says, "Alley, it's the finish line!" People are in the pathway; she clears them out. I "sprint." Can't hear name or cheers. Confused. Everything in slow motion. Some guy touches my shoulders. I say, "I'm okay thanks I can walk." Todd smiles, "Congratulations, honey, you did it!" "No I didn't. I missed the cutoff!" Todd shows me the medal that's around my neck. I AM an Ironman! It turns out the guy who I thought was just touching my shoulders to support me was actually hanging the medal around my neck.

12:15 A.M.: I sit down next to Lynee, glad it's not a bike seat. She says, "Your team is amazing. You're lucky to have them and Coach Wayne. I couldn't have done it without you." I know how she feels. I couldn't have made it without the team either.

1:30 A.M.: Coach Wayne and Todd walk the three bikes back to the Ramada Inn and I hitch a ride with a race official. I tell him I'm surprised I got a medal. He smiles, "Medals are given out through 12:15 A.M.. After THAT it's considered a DNF (did not finish).

2:00 A.M.: Take ice bath for 20 minutes for swelling and aches. My head! Just two blisters; how lucky is that? Feels like jet lag, flu, and hangover.

Monday 10:00 A.M.: At the team celebration brunch Coach Wayne says he got choked up when he saw that the team had waited for me (the last teammate) to cross the finish line! He says we're like wolves–independent, but travel in packs and take care of each other. I can't capture in words how I feel, but I can say that I'm proud to be a part of something so extraordinary. It will always have a place in my heart. ∎

*Alison Boudreau*

# Forever Changed

*My experience with cancer has left me forever changed. Once an athletic superstar, high school honors student, and energetic teenager, my goals have shifted. Today I have something new to live up to:* **I'm a cancer survivor.**

Bang! Boom! Crackle! The fireworks lit up the dark early morning sky and the sea of runners shifted forward. My mom and I floated in a sea of color. We were surrounded by hundreds of people, many of whom were wearing the familiar purple Team In Training jerseys. I thought, "I've come a long way. Thirty months ago I was lying in Boston Children's Hospital struggling to survive. Now I'm starting a 13.1-mile trek through Walt Disney World. This is incredible!"

When I entered high school in 1998, I had everything going for me. I was one of the top 25 students in my class, a high-level figure skater, a competitive soccer player, and one of only 18 girls in my age group selected for Connecticut's Olympic Development Program. I planned to attend college and go places with my soccer and skating.

In February 1999, cancer changed everything. I was diagnosed with non-Hodgkin's lymphoblastic lymphoma my freshman year of high school and I thought the world had ended.

I spent 20 weeks in Boston Children's Hospital, received two years of chemotherapy and cranial radiation, and suffered two major strokes. From day one I suffered terrible headaches and nausea. I lost more than 30 pounds and could not stay awake for long periods. My first week home from the hospital, I developed a blood clot in my brain. I was rushed back to Children's Hospital. Over the course of the next five weeks, I experienced three seizures, encephalopathy, and cranial nerve palsy in my left eye. The night before I was to return home again, the doctors discovered a massive bleed in my brain. I fell into a coma and a shunt had to be placed in my head to drain the built-up blood. I don't remember the next five days, which I spent in the ICU. During the following three weeks the complications did not subside. I developed a staff infection in my shunt and a severe sinus infection. The right side of my body was affected by the bleed in my brain. I had little balance or coordination and needed months of physical therapy. The neuropsychologist found that I had cognitive deficits with my recall and short-term memory. The strokes and seizures had caused permanent brain damage.

The doctors determined that my initial complications were due to my treatment. They changed my chemotherapy and placed me on a new protocol. My body, however, did not handle the new medicine well and a severe toxic reaction put me back in the hospital for another 10 days. There, I suffered from hives, fluid retention, jaundice, and high fevers. Following this reaction, my doctors placed me on low-dose chemotherapy for the remaining 16 months of treatment.

By February of 2000, I was eager to return to my way of life before cancer. My doctors would no longer permit me to play competitive soccer, so instead I turned to figure skating. It took me nearly nine months to regain the balance, coordination, and confidence that I needed to start jumping again. It was halfway through my sophomore year that I returned to school part-time. Over the following two summers, I worked with tutors to make up for the year of school I'd missed. To my delight, as a junior, I was accepted into the National Honors Society. I am proud to say that I graduated **with my class** in June 2002.

I am now one year off chemotherapy and it's been three years since my last stroke. Although cancer took two years of my life away from me, it's given me much more in return. It has forced me to grow emotionally and I am a stronger, more courageous person because of it.

The things I have learned from my cancer experience will forever impact my life. It's unbelievable how many innocent lives are lost to cancer. I've learned that it's not just people on television, in books, or in the newspaper; it's the friends I shared my hospital room with, sat beside in the clinic waiting room, and spent time with at camp. They are bubbly and outgoing like Ginny, who passed away at the age of four. They are beautiful and smart like Naomi and Izzy, who never got the chance to finish high school. They are people who never reached the light at the end of the tunnel. Like all teens with cancer, I've been on an emotional roller coaster—one that hasn't stopped moving, and probably never will.

After facing my own mortality and that of my friends, I have reorganized my priorities. I discovered a love for public speaking, especially that which promotes cancer awareness. I also realized that I deeply enjoy working with children. The positive responses I receive when working with other young cancer patients have encouraged me to pursue a career that involves children.

Volunteering and fund-raising have become a huge part of my life. I am now a teen mentor for several cancer organizations as well as an honored patient for The Leukemia & Lymphoma Society's Team In Training program. Through the clinic and camps, I have spent a lot of time with cancer patients, many of them children. We all have a special bond. The past two summers I took part in Boston's Jimmy Fund Clinic's promotion with Burger King. I was pictured along with four other kids in over 300 Burger Kings in New England. I told my "cancer story" on the radio and at Burger King management meetings to help promote the cause. This past December, both Burger King and the Jimmy Fund Clinic nominated me to carry the Olympic Torch. I was selected and flown to Miami. It was an unbelievable experience and the people I met were truly inspirational! Just thinking about it brings a huge smile to my face! Following my trip, Burger King and Coca-Cola presented me with an amazing gift. They flew both my sister and me to Salt Lake City to attend the last four days of the Winter Olympics! We had an unforgettable time!

My experience with cancer has left me forever changed. Once an athletic superstar, high school honors student, and energetic teenager, my goals have shifted. Today I have something new to live up to: I'm a cancer survivor.

My mom looked over at me as we made our way around the last curve of the race. I clenched her hand and TOGETHER we crossed the finish line. Although the Walt Disney World Half Marathon was long and hard, what we were most proud of was not the marathon itself, but the journey that led us there. ■

*Ashlee Moskwa*

# Dr. Chad Marvel

*When I hear the coming storm and I'm too afraid to even see, you would always know just what to say, you gave your strength to me.*

*You Give Me the Courage*
A song, by Michael Inks, in memory of Chad Marvel

On April 24, 1994, while I was out of town on business, I received an urgent message—call home. An eerie feeling came over me, the kind you have when you know something's not right. Chad, my 14-year-old stepson, hadn't felt well since returning from a school trip to Hawaii. Was he alright, I wondered? I called home and heard the news—Chad had just been diagnosed with chronic myelogenous leukemia (CML), a very resistant form of leukemia. When the doctors told us they wanted to do a bone marrow transplant, we were rocked to our foundation. After catching my breath, I thought, we can beat this.

The transplant went well. Chad was out of the hospital within one month and back in school for the second semester of his sophomore year. He was limited on what he could do and the amount of people he could be around. Chad had been so impacted by professional golfer Paul

Azinger's battle with lymphoma that he and his mom began playing golf in the fall. In the spring, he made the high school golf team.

In the fall of 1994 we became aware of Team In Training. Chad was contacted about being a patient honoree for Debbie Eck, who was going to run a marathon in Hawaii. Over the next few TNT events, Chad would be a patient honoree to many runners. TNT was small, and each runner/walker had their own patient honoree.

During a follow-up visit to check on the transplant's success, we learned that the leukemia was still present. The doctors began new protocols, but they didn't slow Chad down at all. He began his junior year looking forward to the golf season. Even though the leukemia wasn't responding to treatment, when golf season arrived, Chad again made the team. But this season would be different: Chad would be going through more chemo. Not one to give in, Chad continued to play, despite not feeling 100 percent. While the IHSAA granted Chad permission to ride in a cart during matches, Chad walked just like the other players. Despite urging from his mother, Betty, and his coach, and only after his treatments made it impossible for him to walk the course, did he relent and agree to ride. Chad played the entire season! He also won the "Mental attitude award."

In May of 1996, TNT called again. Susan Rockafellow was training for the Anchorage Marathon, had raised double her amount, and wanted to take Chad, her patient honoree, with her. Betty and I joined him, not really knowing what to expect. What we found totally changed our concept of TNT. Of the 2,700 runners in the marathon, 2,600 were TNT members, unified for one cause. We attended the pre-race pasta party, the race, and the victory party, and were amazed at the dedication, compassion, and commitment of everyone we met. They came from all walks of life. They were, for the most part, not elite athletes, just people who cared.

During the race, Chad decided he'd run the Anchorage Marathon the following year. He'd completed the Indianapolis Mini-Marathon less than a year before he was diagnosed, so we figured, why not?

But life had other plans.

On Christmas Eve, 1996, we received the dreaded news that Chad's leukemia was still active and that he'd need another transplant, right away. Knowing he wouldn't be able to run the marathon in June, I signed up in his place. Up to this point, my idea of a long run was from first base to third base.

Chad entered the hospital in January 1997 for his second transplant. This time would be riskier, since his body had already been stressed from the first transplant. Chad had his transplant, went home, and things looked good. But after a few days, complications arose. Chad went back into the hospital. This time, he did not get better.

On Monday, March 31, 1997, a day we'll never forget, the doctors said there was nothing else they could do. Chad wasn't going to make it. Our world stopped. This couldn't be happening! But it was. Chad had given it everything he had, but the leukemia and treatments had taken their toll.

With this news, I told Chad's stepbrothers, Nick and Adam, that Chad wouldn't survive, and we shed many tears. Nick, only two weeks older than Chad, couldn't speak, and wrote down his thoughts. He said Chad had always wanted to be a doctor, and wondered if anybody could make him one. I took Nick's note to the doctors expecting a certificate or something. They did one better. On Wednesday, April 2, 1997, Chad Marvel received an Honorary Doctor of Medicine Degree from the Indiana University School of Medicine. He had made it! Chad was a doctor.

On Sunday, April 6, 1997, Chad succumbed to the complications from his second transplant and passed away.

But that's not the end of our story. I kept training and raising money in Chad's honor. While he was in the hospital, we agreed that the fundraising goal set by TNT wasn't enough and we'd raise $20,000. We raised $26,000! When the marathon came, I finished, with Chad in my heart, in a blazing 6 hours and 12 minutes. Since we'd reached our goal so quickly, we decided we'd do more. As a family, we agreed we'd raise $100,000 in Chad's memory. He never got the chance to practice medicine, but we'd raise enough money in his memory to make a real impact.

Betty signed up and completed the Honolulu Marathon in 1997. Since then, the entire family has completed at least one marathon and, collectively, we've completed eight. Betty, Adam, and I, with close friends Dale and Brenda Whitt, completed the inaugural Rock 'n' Roll Marathon in 1998, and in 1999, Nick, his wife Sara, and I completed the Honolulu Marathon.

In 2001, we went back to Anchorage, where it all began. Sara and I ran with a family friend, Betty mentored, and Nick went as support. Remember our $100,000 goal? We reached it and then some, raising more than $115,000. I ran the Indianapolis Mini-Marathon on May 4, 2002, and in June, 2002, we held our 5th Annual Chad's Challenge Golf

Tournament in memory of Chad and to support The Leukemia & Lymphoma Society's program.

Chad impacted just about everyone he came in contact with. After he died, Mike Inks and Andy Spolyar, two of Chad's friends, wrote a song entitled *You Give Me the Courage*.* The words capture Chad's courage, determination, spirit, and unconditional love for his family and friends. To me, it's not just about Chad, but about every leukemia patient. Before the start of each marathon, I listen to the song. It reminds me of the courage Chad had and gives me the inspiration to continue my mission.

Many people have asked why we keep going, putting our bodies through the trials of a marathon. We do it for Chad, we do it for the survivors, and we do it so other families won't lose what we already have. ■

*Barry Bouse, with Betty, Adam, Nick, and Sara*

---

*You can hear *You Give Me the Courage*, by Michael Inks, at *www.goalsuccess.com*.

# Running Through Grief

*I will keep running and I will survive also.*
*The joy of the run, the joy that is life, continues.*

Allen won't be here to drive me over the Verrazano Bridge to Staten Island to the start of the New York Marathon this year. My sixty-eight-year-old body balks a bit now while I train but I still yearn for the exhilaration of finishing at least one more marathon. In marathoning, to finish is to win. While running in the cooling rain this August morning I thought of the marathon in '86 when finishing was winning in a very special way.

Allen survived to share that marathon day with me. He made it through the first horrible onslaught of chemotherapy after the diagnosis of leukemia in July of '85 when he was 54 years old.

Running sustained me. I lived in Allen's sterile hospital room that first summer of intense treatment. Wearing all white and face masks, the nurses and doctors and I struggled to help Allen. With ice rubs as tortuous to Allen as the raging fever, we tried to cool his burning body. The poison injected through the port in his chest to kill the cancer cells also destroyed his immunity to infection.

Daily I ran. I ran out through the hospital corridors into the streets of New Haven. I ran and I gained strength.

In September of '85 Allen came home from the hospital, a skeleton of himself. And I ran. The school year began and I taught and I ran. The tension, the anxiety of Allen's condition, and the prognosis were overwhelming. I left the house each day to pound the certainty of the earth, to absorb the changes of the seasons, to fill my lungs with the good air, to keep strong for my husband and my children and me, to exult in my ability to keep putting one foot in front of the other no matter what. Running kept me on course. I ran through that fall, that winter, that spring, that summer of '86 and the next fall and Allen ran with me in my heart.

After a year and a half of hospitalization, chemotherapy, spontaneous bleeding, middle of the night emergency room visits, innumerable blood and platelet transfusions, bone marrow tests, and the daily anxiety of uncertain blood counts, Allen was in remission, having outlived his life sentence by a year.

One day while I ran a thought came to me. I would run the New York Marathon and raise money for The Leukemia Society of America. I wrote a letter telling of my mission to friends and relatives thinking I might raise a couple hundred dollars. Allen was a bit embarrassed at first but when the notes and money began pouring in, he got into the spirit. The project mushroomed. Allen became the accountant, totaling up the pledges and enjoying the accompanying notes of love and encouragement. Often confined to home with low blood levels, Allen savored the daily mail. He read and counted and I ran.

It was marathon day in '86. Allen wasn't feeling tip top, but he was well enough to go to New York with me. Allen drove me over the Verrazano Bridge and he kissed me. I hopped out of the car to join the hordes of runners crowding onto Staten Island to prepare for the start. Allen looked pale and he was anxious that I would be all right. It is a long way, 26.2 miles. I was confident and imbued with my mission.

I wore a shirt that said, LUCY AGAINST LEUKEMIA. While I ran through all the boroughs of New York, I surveyed the crowd and handed out little self-made solicitations for our cause. I ran. I flew. I floated. Nothing could stop me.

At the 16-mile mark, just over the Queens borough Bridge on First Avenue and 65th Street, my family was waiting and I paused for hugs and kisses. Two of my four sons joined me in Central Park to run the last two miles. Allen watched the marathon on TV from a hotel room. We were both heroes that day. He was alive and I finished the marathon and raised over $20,000 to fight leukemia.

Allen died a month later.

A giant wave of loss kept catching up with me and enveloping me. I cried and I ran.

One day Bruce Cleland from Harrison, New York, called me. His two-year-old daughter, Georgia, had leukemia. He and his wife Isobel organized a team of runners in the New York Marathon to raise money to fight leukemia called Team In Training. I joined his effort. The team raised more than $300,000 that year.

Since that time I have run many marathons. I have competed in the Senior Olympics on the state and national levels in road races, track, shot put, and discus, always wearing my purple TNT shirt as I continue to dedicate my efforts to fight leukemia and related diseases. In 1996 I received The Leukemia Society's National Chairman's Citation Award for my efforts. To date I have raised nearly $200,000.

I will run again, more slowly now, but keeping one foot in front of the other. I will run in memory of Allen and also in memory of Dan Shapiro, my friend Ruth's husband who also died of leukemia. I will run also in honor of John Engdahl, my hero who survived what Allen and Dan could not because of the progress in treating leukemia. He had an autologous bone marrow transplant and went on to run eight Boston marathons. Progress has been made in the battle against leukemia. John has survived.

I will keep running and I will survive also. The joy of the run, the joy that is life, continues. ∎

*Lucy De Vries Duffy*

# Just For Me

Run run run!
 Have lots of fun!
Try real hard—just for me.
 Make your destination,
It takes lots of concentration.
 So do your best just for me.
Try to find a cure,
 so things won't be a blur
between us and that horrible
disease, so do your very best.
 I'll miss you but I wish
you the best, so do it
 just for me.

     *—Amy Fitzgerald*
     *Age 10*

# I Will Continue

*This is the beginning of a new day. God has given me this day to use as I will. I can waste it or use it for good. What I do today is important because I'm exchanging a day of my life for it. When tomorrow comes, this day will be gone forever; leaving in its place something that I have traded for it. I want it to be a gain, not loss; good, not evil; success, not failure; in order that I shall not regret the price I paid for it.*

W. Heartsill Wilson

When I started exercising, this quote meant nothing to me. At the time, I was 34-years-old, overweight (245 lbs.), traveling, and smoking cigars. I had this idea that I could start running around a bit and "get into shape." Why not? I'd seen a lot of people out running and, frankly, it didn't look too difficult. Just get a pair of shoes—any old shoes would do—and hit the road. Right? I even set a goal for myself. It was, "I will be able to run all the way from my house to the end of our street and back." Yep, all the way to the end of the street and back. One mile. 5,280 feet. No stopping. Continuous motion.

It took me six months.

Next, I thought, "How about the Peachtree Road Race in Atlanta?" It's a 10K, a whopping 6.2 miles! Well, while you won't find my name in the record books under winner, I did finish the Peachtree in one hour and seven minutes.

Now that I was a "real runner," I started training for the Atlanta Half Marathon, held on Thanksgiving Day. That would be the pinnacle of my running career. After crossing the finish line, I'd look out over the crowd gathered at my feet and say, "Mere mortals, I've heard about the 5K's and 10K's that y'all have run, but I ran a half marathon."

As fate would have it, I never ran that half marathon. My family and I accepted a job transfer to North Carolina and, as a result, I stopped running. About a year later, when I did start training again, I heard about an organization that trains people to run marathons; all you have to do is raise money to help their cause. I figured I'd raise the money and, at the ripe old age of 41, run 26.2 miles and prove that I was again at the top of my game.

So in the summer of 2001 I went to a meeting of The Leukemia & Lymphoma Society and signed up to run the Walt Disney World Marathon on January 6, 2002. I was told I'd be running in honor of a young women named Lisa James. Lisa had been diagnosed with acute lymphocytic leukemia (ALL) when she went for her six-week check-up after giving birth to her daughter, Logan. Around the same time, I read an article about a 16-year-old girl named Kimberly Holmes who had just been diagnosed with chronic myelogenous leukemia (CML). I got permission to run in her honor, as well. Fine. I was going to raise money and run a marathon in honor of two young ladies. Where do I start?

I e-mailed people at work, started receiving donations, and in no time had raised enough money to run the marathon. I'd said in my fundraising letter that I would train diligently, increase awareness for The Leukemia & Lymphoma Society, and provide everyone with training updates. No problem. I was going to run a marathon. People would gasp in awe when they saw me run by. I would be like a leaf blowing in the wind: Mr. Effortless in Motion. Did I mention that I weighed 245 pounds?

The training outline didn't look too challenging. Short runs on Tuesdays and Thursdays, a long run on Saturday, and then a three-mile recovery run on Sunday. Hey, wait just a minute, who ever heard of running 3 miles to recover? My idea of recovering is lying on the couch and eating potato chips while watching an old western on TV. Oh well, no problem. After all, I'd already completed the 6.2-mile Peachtree Road Race and I was a runner.

There's an amazing thing about running mileage. It's never too far on paper, but when you get on the road, those Saturday morning runs get *long* fast. By the time we got to 10-mile runs, I wasn't in the shape I thought I'd be and I was getting worried about how I'd handle the rest of those pesky "little" 16.2 miles. The good news was that I'd slimmed down to a petite 235 pounds, so I was sure that things would get easier. But just in case, I decided to prepare for the worst. I went to my Leukemia & Lymphoma Society chapter and picked up some extra Team In Training t-shirts to train in. I figured that if one day I was dying out on a training run, my rescuers would know that at least it was for a good cause. But there was a small kink in my plan. One of the shirts I picked up was an X-large and the other was an XX-large. My son Adam, who was five, could wear the X-large. This was a bit disconcerting, considering I'd indicated *my* shirt size was X-large when I signed up for the program. I hoped they didn't expect me to wear something that small during the marathon. I'm sure there's some kind of law that forbids fat men from wearing kids' t-shirts while participating in sporting events. If not, there ought to be. Oh well, I'd just keep running.

And then came September 11, 2001.

Our entire team was still shell-shocked when we met on Saturday, September 15, for our scheduled 8-mile training run. More team members showed up for that run than any other run during our training. It was by far one of the toughest runs for everyone. Many people complained of not having been able to sleep all week, but still they said it felt important to get out there with everyone else. If nothing else, just to run and to think. And thinking is something I'd been doing a lot of as well. I made a few post- September 11 attack resolutions. They can all be pretty well summed up in one word—CONTINUE. I'd like to share them with you:

I will CONTINUE to kiss my son every chance I get. And when he gets too big for that mushy stuff (which I fear is not too far off), I will resort to hugging him. And if that starts to embarrass him, I'll just put my arm around his shoulder, but I will do everything I can to show him that I love him.

I will CONTINUE to teach Adam, in the best way I know how, the difference between right and wrong, how much it means to be responsible for his actions, and how important it is that he show respect for others, no matter who they are or what they look like.

I will CONTINUE to hold my wife, kiss her, and tell her I love her every morning before I go to work. She is still the most beautiful woman I know and I am forever grateful that she is in my life.

I will CONTINUE to try to help those less fortunate than I, whether it be in the form of my church tithe, donations to the United Way, or running a marathon to raise money for leukemia. God has blessed me and my family, and I want to share that with others.

I will CONTINUE and I hope you will too.

And now back to my training.

I picked up a real running partner, not someone recovering from an injury. Ted Budd could have run at least a minute per mile faster, but he didn't go off and leave an old fat man struggling for his last breath on the side of the road. Actually, I begged him to leave me. It's hard to stop when someone's dragging you along. Ya'll know what I mean. Like eating the cookie when no one's looking. Doesn't count if no one sees.

Speaking of cookies, let me tell you something unbelievable. I am probably the only person who has ever gained weight while training for a marathon. I started off losing about 23 pounds, but I gained back five of them. That's right boys and girls; I managed to beat all the odds and gain weight. Ever hear of Gummy Bears? Unfortunately, I have, and I've found that they're quite tasty during long runs. Alright, I can't blame it all on the bears. I have increased my eating to about three times what a normal person should require to survive. I keep telling myself it's alright to have that candy bar because I'm going to "run it off" tomorrow. Well, it won't be much longer now; the marathon is just around the corner. All of my training is going to pay off and I will emerge a marathoner. I will have reached my goal. When my friends ask me if I'd like to go out for a run, I'll just look at them and say, "Huh, you wouldn't last 10 miles."

**26.2 Miles—5:20:34**

I did it. I completed a marathon. Better than that, I now understand what the quote at the beginning means. I could sit here and write about how early I had to get up on race day to be at the starting line. Or tell you about the cold rain that started around mile 10, and lasted until mile 13.

Or how my legs felt like lead around mile 20. Or about rounding the corner and finally seeing the finish line after plodding along for five hours and thirty minutes. I could tell you that I, Mike Fitzpatrick, completed a *marathon.*

BUT SO WHAT?

If I told you about all of those things, I wouldn't be telling you what the marathon meant to me. So instead, I'd like to tell you about standing in the starting corral before the sun came up and seeing the picture of a small happy child pinned to a woman's back with the words "In Memory of Macennah—My Little Angel." Or about the gentleman I saw at mile 12 with cerebral palsy, putting one foot in front of the other the best way he could. Or the courage on a father's face as he stood in front of a crowded room and read the "Ten Life Lessons" that his daughter, Kimberly Joy Costa (July 17, 1981–July 24, 2000), had written for her high school graduation. Or the thank you note from Kimberly Holmes telling me about her recent blood work and how the doctor said it was great. I can type these words, or tell you about each instance, but I'll never be able to describe to you the feelings associated with each one.

And you know what? I'm pretty sure it's a good thing I can't. I believe there are certain feelings no one should ever be able to capture in words. To do so would be an injustice. You need to stand there and feel the tears rolling down your cheeks yourself. Then you'll understand.

I will never regret the price that I paid for January 6, 2002. I ran a marathon. My race is over. For Lisa James and Kimberly Holmes and many others like them, their race continues. I pray that they win. ∎

*Mike Fitzpatrick*

# The Challenge Continues

*I will be with you every step of the way.*

When I first told my friends and family that I was going to run an ultramarathon—anything beyond 26.2 miles—they said, "You're going to run how far? In one day? Are you crazy? Have you lost your mind?"

Their reactions illustrate just how far out there people think you have to be to run ultramarathons. And you know what, they're probably right. In addition to patience, these races require the ability to suffer, both physically and mentally. My answer to my friends and family was, "What better way to honor my friend and honored patient Matt Lewis?" I'll get back to the ultramarathon in a minute, but first let me tell you how I ended up making the decision to run it in the first place.

I'd been a competitive runner for many years. I'd even achieved a measure of success, having the opportunity to run for the ASICS shoe company in 1990 and 1991. However, when 1992 rolled around, I was burnt out: I'd lost my love for running. I felt I had accomplished everything I'd set out to do as a runner. So, I hung up my running shoes and moved on to other things.

It wasn't until late 1997 that I realized there was still one running goal I wanted to achieve—running the Boston Marathon. I decided to start training for a marathon where I could qualify for the 1999 Boston Marathon.

Shortly after I started training, I attended an informational meeting for Team In Training. I went to the meeting not really knowing what to expect. After listening to several people speak about the program, I still wasn't completely sold. Then, an 11-year-old boy who was battling leukemia got up in front of the room and talked about what it meant to him to have complete strangers run hundreds of miles to train for a marathon in order to help kids like him. The boy who spoke at the meeting was Matt Lewis. His words encouraged me to sign up for the program.

It turned out that Matt lived in my neighborhood and he was assigned as my patient hero. I didn't know Matt or his family prior to meeting him at the informational meeting, but I signed up for the 1998 Suzuki Rock 'n' Roll Marathon in San Diego and trained to run it in his honor. I had no idea at the time just how much of an impact Matt would have on my life.

Matt was a typical seven-year-old boy when he was diagnosed with chronic myelogenous leukemia (CML) in April of 1994. CML rarely occurs in children (only four percent of childhood leukemias are CML). The only consistently successful curative treatment for CML has been high-dose chemotherapy and total-body radiation, followed by a bone marrow transplant. So, Matt endured the chemotherapy and radiation and, following that, he had a successful bone marrow transplant. Matt's younger brother Greg, two-years-old at the time, was his marrow donor.

When I met Matt in 1998, he'd been in remission for almost four years. He enjoyed playing ice hockey and little league baseball. He had even run a couple of 5K races. We hit it off from the start. I was able to teach him a little about running when he joined me for some of my shorter training runs. And I learned a great deal from him as well. Matt taught me the true meaning of courage, strength, and compassion. These are lessons that will remain with me forever.

Conditions were brutal the day of the 1998 Suzuki Rock 'n' Roll Marathon in San Diego. It was hot and humid and there wasn't enough drinking water on the course. In the latter stages of the race, I became dehydrated and my legs began cramping. Every step I took was more painful than the last. In an attempt to shift my focus off the pain, I thought about the poster Matt had made for my trip. It said, "I will be with you every step of the way." I began to think about everything Matt had experienced in his short life. My pain and suffering were immediately put into perspective. Matt was with me. Just like on our weekend training runs, he was right beside me. I realized that, while I was slowing down, I still had to reach my goal of qualifying for Boston, for Matt as much as myself. With Matt's inspiration, I finished the race exhausted and dehydrated in 3 hours and 6 minutes. That finish was good enough to qualify me for the 1999 Boston Marathon with a little over three minutes to spare.

I had my official marathon finisher's medal engraved with both Matt's and my name on it. I was excited to give the medal to Matt since he'd been my inspiration for qualifying for Boston. But when I arrived at Matt's house to give him the medal, my excitement evaporated. While I was in San Diego, Matt had gone to Children's Hospital for a routine check-up only to learn that after nearly four years in remission, his leukemia was back. He had suffered a relapse. While I'd been conditioning my body over the past months to reach its physical peak, Matt's body had been under assault by this horrible disease. I felt helpless and angry. Even so, I could only imagine what Matt and his family were feeling. I decided to do the only thing I could—I would run the Boston Marathon in Matt's honor.

My 33rd birthday fell on the same day as the 1999 Boston Marathon. I remember standing at the starting line with 12,000 of the world's best marathoners, thinking how lucky I was to be there. And then, bang, the starter's gun fired and we were off and running in the 103rd Boston Marathon. The crowd support was amazing. The streets were lined with more than 1.5 million spectators. There wasn't an open spot along either side of the road for the entire 26.2 miles.

The race was even more special because Matt and his family had traveled to Boston to share the experience with me. I knew that Matt would be at the 17-mile mark. As I approached that point in the race, I didn't think I would ever find him in the mob of people lining the street. But suddenly, up ahead, a young boy ran out of the crowd and onto the race course. I couldn't believe it . . . it was Matt! He'd been the first person to spot me coming up the road and he wanted to let me know that I had his support. He extended his hand for a high-five and then ran with me for about 50 yards. At that moment, I understood the true meaning of the marathon and of Team In Training. This wasn't just a race. It was a celebration of life and a celebration of hope . . . the hope that we will find a cure for leukemia so that Matt and the thousands of other kids like him will be able to live long healthy lives. The smile on Matt's face as he ran beside me provided all the strength I needed to make it to the finish line. I completed the Boston Marathon in 2 hours and 52 minutes. My finishing time put me in the top three and a half percent overall. The best part of the Boston Marathon, however, was running for Matt and with Matt and raising $8,600 for The Leukemia & Lymphoma Society. I couldn't have asked for a better birthday gift.

Not long after the marathon, I received some fantastic news—Matt was back in remission! Matt has continued to inspire me. Largely because of him, I have become even more involved with The Leukemia & Lymphoma Society. I was honored to be nominated to the board of trustees for the Western Pennsylvania and West Virginia chapter in 1999 and still hold that position today. I also helped create the Team In Training bicycling program for our local chapter. I serve as the head cycling coach for our chapter and our cycling teams have raised more than $500,000.

As for the ultramarathon, what an experience! The ultramarathon I'd signed up for was a 56.4-mile race (a double marathon) in the Colorado Rocky Mountains. As if 56.4 miles is not difficult enough at sea level, this race took place at an elevation of 9,000 feet.

I don't think I have ever been so nervous before a race. Everything about it was new to me: the distance, the terrain, and the altitude. I had also learned at the event registration that I was the only rookie ultramarathoner participating in the race. It wasn't long into the race before I realized I was in for a challenging day. The race course was a true wilderness trail, complete with log piles and other obstacles to negotiate. In addition, there was a swampy area, so my feet were wet from mile five to the finish. This had the added bonus of giving me painful blisters. The hills were tougher than expected too, with a real punishing one at the 8-mile mark. Since I had to run four laps on a 13.1-mile loop, this grueling hill showed up at miles 8, 21, 34, and 47.

The first three laps (39 miles) weren't too bad. However, into the final lap (13.1 miles), I knew I was going to have to dig deep to get to the finish line. Despite being the only rookie in the race, and having done very little altitude training, I had one big advantage over my competitors—I had Matt Lewis. When the pain in my legs became almost unbearable, I thought about the pain Matt had endured. Matt has taught me that the human spirit is capable of miracles. Now it was my turn to show him that I had learned the lesson well. I focused every ounce of energy I had into putting one foot in front of the other. As the final miles passed under my feet, I thought about the children I have met over the past few years who have lost their battles with cancer. This 52.4-mile endurance test was for them too. The finish line was now in sight. I had made it. And to top it off, I finished in fourth place.

While preparing for the ultramarathon, I raised $12,009 for Team In Training. Since 1998, I have raised nearly $40,000, thanks to the generosity of many people. What's next? I'm not sure. But stay tuned: my finishing time in the ultramarathon qualified me for the Western States 100-mile run with well over one and a half hours to spare. One hundred miles of running seems quite daunting, but I know this much: with Matt Lewis as my inspiration, anything is possible! ■

*Tim Hamburger*

# Remembering the Reason

## Chris' Story

*They stopped to eat, stopped to rest, stopped to drink, but they didn't stop moving forward. All 19 students and 5 adults crossed the finish line . . .*

O ur son, Christopher Austin Beemer, was born on July 3, 1983, to celebration and fireworks. The same atmosphere that heralded his arrival would, in the years that followed, be a focal point of his birthdays. Two years later, we were blessed with a daughter on October 9, 1985. We felt our family was complete. While my husband and I had busy careers, our children were our lives.

Chris was an active, energetic child who loved being outdoors, especially in winter. While he played and watched many sports, he especially loved football and ice hockey. In the winter, when our pond froze, Chris shoveled it so he could skate and play hockey with his friends.

During the summer he turned 14 in 1997, Chris delivered newspapers so he could save money to buy a snow blower. We could've bought him one, but we wanted him to learn how to set goals and manage his money and we thought this would be a good lesson. But Chris never saw another winter.

The first weekend in September 1997, a week into eighth grade, Chris was named starting center for his school's football team, a great honor. But when the first game arrived, Chris didn't play but instead sat on the sidelines. After the game, Chris said he'd told the coach he wasn't feeling well and that he couldn't play. When we got home, I took his temperature. It was 102. It wasn't unusual for kids to get a "bug" at the beginning of the school year, so we were sure this would pass.

For most of the next week, Chris remained sick and we kept him home. After one visit to the doctor, we took him back for a blood test. The doctor knew mono was going around and we assumed that was the problem.

I can't begin to describe our shock and fear on September 12, 1997, when the doctor called with Chris' test results—he thought Chris had leukemia. We'd heard of it and knew it was a blood disorder, but we didn't know it was a deadly cancer. Our doctor immediately put Chris in the hospital for a spinal tap and bone marrow test. Needless to say, life changed forever with that call.

By 1:00 P.M. that fateful Friday, Chris was diagnosed with acute lymphocytic leukemia (ALL). We were numb, scared, devastated, and overwhelmed by the news and how much we had to learn about this disease and our treatment options. We also needed to support Chris and be there for our daughter as she struggled to understand what was happening. We were advised that Chris was at higher risk because he was older than age 10. We had no idea what was to follow. I'll never forget the phone call I made to Chris' coach to explain why Chris wouldn't be at practice. It wasn't until I said it out loud that it became real and I was reduced to uncontrollable sobs of panic and fear.

Chris remained hospitalized and the testing and chemotherapy began. I worked at Sparrow Hospital in Lansing, Michigan, where Chris was being treated, so I was confident he would get the best care. His physicians consulted with experts around the country, and I could effectively advocate for him because I knew his caregivers and knew how to navigate the health care system. For any patient or family touched by leukemia, you know of the pain that accompanies the fevers, rashes, endless needle pokes, blood transfusions, chemotherapy, spinal taps, cat scans, MRI's, ultrasounds, and worse involved in the treatment of this disease. This is in addition to the daily stress and strain of the mental and emotional roller coaster.

While Chris was hospitalized, he became septic, developed significant abdominal pain, and, as a last resort, underwent two major abdominal surgeries to try to remove infected organs and tissue. He came out of surgery on a ventilator and in a drug-induced coma. On October 28, 1997, after a courageous six-and-a-half-week battle, Chris passed away with his family, grandparents, aunts, uncles, and cousins at his side. Later, we recognized the significance of the fireworks we watched from his hospital room the night before he died—fireworks marked both the beginning and end of his short life.

In shock like all parents who have lost a child, we fought depression, battled feelings of helplessness at not being able to save him, and tried to pull ourselves together for our daughter, maintain our jobs, and regain some semblance of a feeling of family. We read books on grief and loss, but none described how we felt. We wondered if the numbness would ever subside. We also attended a children's grief and loss support group with our daughter to try to help her express her feelings and talk with other children who'd lost loved ones.

We somehow got through Christmas, Mother's Day, and Father's Day. We especially struggled, though, with the anticipation of what would have been Chris' 15th birthday on July 3, 1998. We spent hours at the cemetery that holiday weekend and were comforted by friends and family who came in support. There was no way we could go to the fireworks celebrations that weekend, and as we sat in our home, we shuddered with the sound of each boom.

Upon returning to work, I received a call from one of Chris' favorite nurses. It had been nine months since we'd spoken, and I was thankful to be able to talk to someone who knew Chris and how he had suffered. She said she'd thought of Chris and the rest of us many times since his death and was about to make a commitment to raise money and train to do a marathon in Chris' memory as part of the Team In Training program. I could hardly speak. Through my tears, she told me the marathon would be in Honolulu, HI, and that she would love it if my husband, daughter, and I could be there to watch her cross the finish line. We were profoundly moved that this nurse, who cared for many children battling cancer, would think of Chris and make this commitment in his memory.

I told her that after feeling helpless at Chris' bedside, and experiencing the feelings of vulnerability that followed, maybe I could do it with her. While I feared I didn't have the emotional stamina to do it and I knew physically that it would be especially challenging, I went with her to a meeting to learn more. By the end of the meeting, I signed up and threw myself into training and fundraising.

It was extremely difficult to talk about Chris and ask people for contributions. But his inspiration helped me overcome my embarrassment over being reduced to tears in front of others. Participating in the Team In Training program gave me something to look forward to and helped me focus on what we could do to honor Chris. It helped us come together as a family as we planned fundraising events together. My training regimen became a positive part of our lives, and we looked forward to going to the Honolulu Marathon that December. We raised over $10,000 for the cause.

As we boarded the plane for Honolulu, we wondered what was to come. Never in my wildest dreams would I have imagined participating in an event requiring such physical endurance. And we still had to get through those awkward moments when we were asked about what had prompted us to be in the program and we couldn't talk about it without making everyone uncomfortable. Still, when we arrived, we were greeted by the friendly, supportive people of the TNT program. Plus, our favorite nurse who "understood" was there, and her enthusiasm and confidence was a tremendous help.

The Honolulu Marathon starts at 5:00 A.M., with people lining up in the cold and darkness. While everyone was in awe of the fireworks display marking the beginning of the race, I was reduced to a puddle of tears as the significance hit me, but I knew Chris was watching and I garnered the mental resolve to get in the race.

Like many other runners and walkers, I attached a picture of Chris to the back of my race jersey. Throughout the race, passers-by shared words of encouragement and gave hugs and other signs of affection as I put one foot in front of the other. When I finished, it not only marked my love for Chris, but also a new beginning for our family. The picture of Chris' favorite nurse and I crossing the finish line together is proudly displayed in my office, and I willingly share the story with anyone who will listen.

Our experience with TNT was so powerful that I continued to train and raise funds for the cause. In 1999, I finished the San Diego Rock 'n Roll Marathon and the Honolulu Marathon. Each time, my joints became more painful and I needed medication to reduce the swelling and pain. I trained less to try to recover, but kept fundraising. Then, when the mother of one of Chris' best friends said she'd do a marathon with me, we started training and fundraising for the Dublin, Ireland, marathon in October 2000.

I wasn't sure whether physically I could do it and my training was less than adequate, but I was determined. I especially wanted to be there for this special friend, who had previously walked with me so many times as I struggled to get out the door. In addition, I was especially touched when the Michigan chapter of The Leukemia & Lymphoma Society asked if I would share "Chris' story" at the pre-race pasta party. I was afraid—on the third anniversary of Chris' death, how could I, in front of a thousand people, share "Chris' story" without uncontrollable sobbing? I knew they were concerned about having me speak because they didn't want it to be "depressing," so I made the speech motivating and inspiring, opening the door for others who had personal experiences to share. I felt proud and was overwhelmed by the heartwarming response.

As I contemplated the prospect of not doing another marathon, I realized how hard it was going to be to watch Chris' friends and teammates go through their senior year of high school. We'd followed the football and ice hockey teams after Chris' death and my heart ached as I watched his friends get driver's licenses, find girlfriends and boyfriends, go to the prom, prepare college admission applications, plan for their senior trip, etc. In addition, there were daily reminders in the mail regarding his class ring, varsity jacket, registration for the armed services, college admissions exams, special deals at the local car dealerships, credit card applications, etc. These reminders were more than we could bear some days.

Since I wasn't sure about my ability to do another marathon, I thought about how I could support others to participate in TNT. Maybe I could enlist a group of Chris' friends to do the Honolulu Marathon in December 2001 in his memory, but there were a lot of issues: These students weren't 18-years-old and couldn't enter into a contract, we'd need more than four to five months to raise funds, different incentives and timelines would be required, chaperones would be needed, etc., etc. I prepared a proposal, had lunch with the executive director of the Michigan chapter of The Leukemia & Lymphoma Society, and made my pitch. She immediately supported me, got approval from the national office, and we embarked on yet another journey of the heart.

I sent out invitations and put up flyers at Holt High School inviting students to meet about forming a team. I was anxious. What if no one came? What if no one found it meaningful to remember Chris in this way? After all, it had been three years since Chris had passed away—these kids were moving on. I prepared myself for heartbreak.

There were twice as many people as I had anticipated. While parents were understandably uneasy, I asked for their patience and faith. I discussed the educational benefits, the prospect of goal setting and achievement, money management, community service, teamwork, and physical endurance, not to mention the emotional fulfillment. The trip to Honolulu was an added plus.

Twenty students signed up (my daughter being one of them). To my surprise, five adults (of whom four were parents of students) also made the commitment! With this many team members, our fundraising goal exceeded $100,000! I told the students if they each raised $1,000, and they as a team raised $20,000, I would raise the remaining $50,000. I hoped vendors and others would provide support with corporate sponsorships.

We embarked on a "marathon" of fundraising, doing pop can drives, car washes, a spaghetti dinner, several pancake breakfasts, a haircut-a-thon, a charity ball, silent auction, candy/bake sales, and school dances. We sold Mary Kay cosmetics and Longaberger gift baskets, helped organize and hold a special "Concert for a Cure," did yard work, and had a booth at the annual summer Holt Hometown Days festival. Some students got summer jobs; others worked concessions at Michigan State University. For eight months we held a fundraising activity or event nearly every weekend. The special mom with whom I'd run the Dublin Marathon and her husband were our account manager and coach, respectively. They devoted countless hours to fundraising and preparing the team.

The students named their team the Holt Team WALL (Working Against Leukemia and Lymphoma). The local television stations and newspapers covered them and announced the team's fundraising events. They worked hard, behaved responsibly, and committed themselves. The funds came slowly, but they came.

Then, on September 11, 2001, while we watched the horror of the terrorists' actions against the U.S., we received a phone call that brought terror closer to home. We learned that one of our team members had been hospitalized that day with a diagnosis of leukemia. How could one of our own be afflicted with this deadly disease? What a terrible irony—this teen, who had made a commitment to fundraise and do a marathon for someone he'd never met (he was a classmate of our daughter but had never met Chris), was now battling the disease himself. How could this be happening again?

The team strengthened their resolve, putting banners on the homecoming float and sponsoring a walk-a-thon in his honor. His father said, "I think you realize what's important and what isn't. Some of the things you used to care about you just don't anymore." We remembered how precious life is.

Fundraising after September 11 became much more difficult. Communities rallied around the national cause and charitable donations were rightfully diverted to relief efforts. The impact on our own fundraising was evident, and we didn't know until the night before we were scheduled to leave how close we were to hitting our target. What a thrill when the final tally revealed that we had done it—we had raised over $100,000! Nineteen students and five adults were ready to run!

We arrived in Honolulu late Friday afternoon on December 7, 2001, and Saturday evening brought all of the excitement, preparation, and fundraising efforts into focus at the pre-race pasta party. We dined with 2,400 other runners, walkers, volunteers, families, and other supporters. We listened to personal stories of pain, struggle, triumph, and loss from families, friends, and survivors of these terrible diseases.

I felt privileged to again be one of the speakers. With photos of Chris behind me, some with him and team members, and pictures from various fundraising activities, I shared "Chris' story" and told them how proud I was of the team. When the crowd gave me a standing ovation, I was overwhelmed. I learned later that any personal doubts that our team harbored had evaporated when I shared our battle with the loss of Chris and the remarkable work of this special team.

Like most first-timers, I'm sure none of them slept a wink that night. They got up at 3:00 A.M. for a team photo in the hotel lobby. Then, after walking to the starting area, the fireworks burst over the Pacific. As I wiped my tears, I watched them take off for the experience of their lives.

Along the way they were given encouragement from many who'd heard their story. They stopped to eat, stopped to rest, stopped to drink, but they didn't stop moving forward. All 19 students and 5 adults crossed the finish line in times ranging between five and nine hours. They collected their medals and t-shirts and headed back to the hotel with sore feet and muscles and the personal satisfaction that only those who complete a marathon know. In marathons, to finish is to win, and on that day, the entire Holt Team WALL, students and adults, were winners.

My family and I continue to raise funds for The Leukemia & Lymphoma Society. Plus, I'm now on the board of directors of the Michigan chapter, my husband is a TNT volunteer coordinator, and our daughter is training and fundraising for another marathon. With Chris as our inspiration, we'll continue our commitment to help find a cure for leukemia in our lifetimes. We hope and pray others will be moved to do the same. ■

*Pamela S. Beemer*

**The amazing students of Team WALL who made the commitment to make a difference are:**

Lindsey Baxter, Class of 2002
Lindsey Beemer, Class of 2004
Sara Benington, Class of 2002
Sara Bilunes, Class of 2002
Jennifer Christensen, Class of 2003
Leah Faleer, Class of 2002
Tom Griffith, Class of 2003
Steve Jenkins, Class of 2002
Billy Kingsley, Class of 2004
    (father died of leukemia in 1997)
Adam LaFeve, Class of 2002
Alissa Lewis, Class of 2002
Maureen Parsons, Class of 2004
Neal Parsons, Class of 2002
Travis Rook, Class of 2004
    (diagnosed with leukemia Sept. 2001)
Dan Smith, Class of 2002
Scott Tedford, Class of 2002
Matt Terrill, Class of 2002
Tommy Terrill, Class of 2003
Anne Wallace, Class of 2002
Amanda Werner, Class of 2002

# The Entertainer

*When you look at Paul and you see his face, or when you listen to him sing and you're in his presence, it's living proof that Team In Training, and The Leukemia & Lymphoma Society are succeeding.*

By age two our son Paul was already an entertainer. Every opportunity he got, whether in front of friends and family or complete strangers, he put on a show. At age four he had a little tuxedo and sang his first full Frank Sinatra song in a restaurant called "Don't Tell Mama" on 46th Street in Manhattan. Everyone could see that he was headed for bright lights.

When Paul was eight, I took him to see the Rosie O'Donnell show. It was an afternoon taping and we arrived early to get good seats. When we got there we joined 100 other people in the lobby. After waiting for close to 45 minutes, we learned that Madonna was with Rosie and that they'd gone out to lunch. The taping would be delayed. While everybody waited for close to two hours, Paul entertained the crowd with Sinatra songs and jokes. Most of the people waiting were women and they all thought Paul was adorable.

Little did we know that Rosie had a warm-up act to keep the crowd entertained before the show. Apparently, every time this guy came out to say something funny or to make sure we weren't getting too restless, Paul was in the middle of a song. He must have said something to Rosie because when the show started she didn't go into her planned routine. Instead, she said, "My warm-up guy tells me that there's a little boy named Paul who can sing Sinatra, and has been entertaining all of you for the last hour and a half. Where's Paul? Paul, come up here." So Paul went up and immediately hit it off with Rosie. He sang Sinatra tunes for her, and it was clear that it was love at first sight, so to speak. We were on a real high after the show.

Less than a week later, Paul began feeling ill. He had swollen glands when we took him to the doctor, but our pediatrician thought it was probably just a sore throat or possibly mono. He told us to come back in two weeks if Paul's glands were still swollen.

A week later, Paul still had a sore throat and he began complaining that it hurt when he swallowed. My wife, Michele, brought him back to the doctor. This time the doctor sent us to a specialist who took blood samples. He informed us that Paul's white blood cell count was extremely low, which was cause for concern. Less than 24 hours later, Paul was diagnosed with leukemia. The next day he received his first dose of chemotherapy. Our world screeched to a halt. We didn't know anything about leukemia. Up until then, to us, cancer meant death. We were numb.

His second day in the hospital the phone rang in Paul's room. It was Rosie O'Donnell. Somebody had called to tell her about Paul. She was shocked to hear that this little boy, who'd been on her show two weeks earlier, had been diagnosed with leukemia. She spoke to Michele and I, but she really called to talk with Paul. They had a great conversation, but we could tell that she was upset.

The following day a big box arrived from FAO Schwartz. It was from Rosie. During her show that day she sent a special get-well message out to "her little buddy Paul." Paul and Rosie remain friends to this day. In the first two years after they met, Paul appeared on her show seven times. In total he was on the show nine times; the final time was during the last week she was on the air. It was touching to see their relationship develop.

After Paul's diagnosis, his doctors laid out the plan for his treatment. It would last for 130 weeks. The treatment would include chemotherapy, regular hospital stays, spinal taps, and oral medication, among other things.

It was a whole lot of treatment for an eight-year-old. Paul's attitude was all that kept us from falling apart. We'd look at Paul, sitting up in his hospital bed with an IV bag dripping chemotherapy into his bloodstream, and watch as he sang, told jokes, and laughed. Watching him, I'd think, how can I, his father, not be positive, when he is so positive?

Don't get me wrong, the cancer treatment was extremely difficult, but Paul took it in stride. There was a period when he had to take a pill called methotrexate every day. He'd take it at bedtime knowing that it was guaranteed to make him feel nauseous the next morning. Even so, he accepted that he had to take the pill and never complained.

During Paul's illness and treatment he continued to perform. When he was diagnosed, he had the lead role in a small community production of *Oliver*. It was an 800-seat theater and he performed two weekends straight, while he was receiving chemotherapy!

Like any father, I wanted to trade places with my son, to take his medicine, take his pain, take his treatment, anything. I was so frustrated that all I could do was hope and pray. And then I heard about Team In Training. I thought to myself, "I can do that." I'd run a marathon prior to Paul getting sick, so I didn't have any doubt that I could run 26.2 miles. If anything, it would be raising the money that would be the challenge, or so I thought.

I wrote a letter from my heart and sent it to everyone we knew and everyone Paul's grandparents knew. What happened after that was truly amazing. Each day I'd return home from work to find a stack of envelopes. In them were donations of every size. One woman I worked with, a single secretary and grandmother on a fixed income, sent us $5.00. That donation held as much meaning to us as the $5,000 check we received. Almost everybody sent something. I couldn't believe what a single letter, what a bunch of words describing what was happening in our lives, could bring. While we were still dealing with the fact that our little boy had cancer, opening those letters each night was a ray of sunshine during our darkest days. We raised more than $101,000 from individual donations—a record.

Thankfully, Paul has stayed in remission since his initial 130 weeks of treatment. Over the next two and a half years, Paul performed continually, including appearing in a K-Mart commercial with Rosie. The Leukemia & Lymphoma Society caught on to the fact that Paul has the ability to speak to and entertain large crowds and they asked him to be a patient ambassador. They flew us to San Diego, Arizona, and Washington state, and Paul spoke to groups ranging from 50 to 5,000 people. He sang the national anthem at one of the Rock 'n' Roll Marathons in front of 14,000 people. To see this little boy get up in front of huge crowds and speak about what was going on in his life and sing his heart out was awesome.

The Leukemia & Lymphoma Society has continued to send Paul to events over the years, including a $500-a-plate fundraiser where he spoke and performed. It's exciting to see him using his talent to promote the blood-related cancer cause. He's a spokesperson for The Leukemia & Lymphoma Society, a patient, and a youth ambassador. He even met Vice President Al Gore. When you look at Paul and you see his face, or when you listen to him sing and you're in his presence, it's living proof that Team In Training and The Leukemia & Lymphoma Society are succeeding. ■

*Anthony Iacono*

# Reminder...

At *www.goalsuccess.com* you can . . .

- Hear Paul Iacono sing
- Browse photos that accompany the stories you've just read
- Find updates on the story contributors and the people they have written about
- Send a message to any of the story contributors
- Read additional inspiring stories

# PART THREE

## Your Success Toolbox

*Step-by-Step Guidance for Developing Your Own Winning GAIN Plans*

*We are each given a block of marble when we begin a lifetime and the tools to shape it into sculpture. We can drag it behind us untouched, we can pound it into gravel, or we can shape it into glory.*

Unknown

# Tools for Developing Winning GAIN Plans

A re you inspired to work towards achieving your important goals? Are you ready to start turning your dreams into reality? Are you ready to create GAIN Plans to make that happen? If so, Part Three will show you how. Part Three, *Your Success Toolbox*, provides the practical how-to information and easy-to-use forms you'll need to develop your own winning GAIN Plans.

Part Three is broken into three sections, *Individual GAIN Planning Tools*, *Team GAIN Planning Tools*, and a bonus section, *Goal Setting Tools for Teens*. Here's a brief description of what you will find in each section.

*Individual GAIN Planning Tools* focuses on creating GAIN Plans for all your individual goals. Whether you want to improve your fitness level, look for a new job, increase your income, or learn to skydive, this section will help you create a GAIN Plan to do it.

*Team GAIN Planning Tools* focuses on creating GAIN Plans for teams. From sports teams to workgroup teams, every team has goals. It's critical that teams spend time discussing their goals and creating plans to reach them. *Team GAIN Planning Tools* includes a list of questions every team should discuss each time they begin to work towards a challenging goal.

*Goal Setting Tools for Teens* is written for today's teens and anyone invested in helping them succeed. It includes guidance for teens to help them determine the important goals in their lives. The centerpiece of this section are the 50, "What I Really Want Out of Life!" questions. These questions are designed to help teens gain clarity about their life's purpose and related goals. This section is ideal for teens who are considering personal, athletic, academic, career, volunteer, and other important goals. I suggest that you encourage any teens in your life to read and do the exercises in this section. It has the power to make a real difference in their future!

# GAIN Planning Forms

The forms in the following sections are intended to be used over and over as you continually set new goals. To this end I have provided you with three different options for reusing these forms.

## Option One—Download Them

All of the forms in the following sections can be downloaded as PDF files from *Inspiration to Perspiration* online at *www.goalsuccess.com*. The downloadable versions of the forms are larger, giving you much more space to write.

## Option Two—Go Digital

If you prefer, you can generate all your GAIN Plans online by following the guidelines on *Inspiration to Perspiration* online. Just answer the questions and print out your completed GAIN Plans. The website also contains information, support, and related services to help ensure that you create and stick to GAIN Plans that will lead to your success.

## Option Three—Reproduce Them

If you do not wish to download the forms or fill them out online, you can use the ones included in the book. I suggest that you photocopy the forms and leave the originals blank for future GAIN Planning. Feel free to photocopy, for your personal use, any form where you see "Downloadable" at the top of the page.

Okay, let's get started developing your winning GAIN Plans.

# Individual GAIN
# Planning Tools

*A thousand mile journey begins with a single step.*

Confucius

*From setting the right goals to choosing the best people to include in your networks of support, if you follow the guidelines in this section, you will be on your way to making your dreams reality.*

If you have read this book straight through or are starting here, you may want to review Part One, Develop Winning GAIN Plans, before you go on. It will refresh you on the components that will make up your GAIN Plan.

When you are ready to start your GAIN Planning process, follow the directions beginning on the next page.

# Individual GAIN Planning Instructions

## Review the Tips

Begin by reviewing the Quick Tips for each of the four GAIN Planning steps. Consider how they apply to the goal you are preparing to set.

## Complete the Forms

After reviewing the *Quick Tips,* use the forms in the remainder of this section to create your GAIN Plans.

The last form is a one-page GAIN Plan Summary sheet. Use it to capture the highlights of your GAIN Plan. Keep the summary sheet close at hand while you work on your goal. Review it on a daily basis.

Good luck, and enjoy the process of reaching your goals.

For more information, additional forms, or coaching go to *Inspiration to Perspiration* online at *www.goalsuccess.com.*

# Quick Tips Review

## Quick Tips for Setting Specific and Challenging Goals

- Commit to the right goals for you
- Set specific, challenging, and tightly focused goals
- Start each goal statement with, "I will..."
- Set goals at the right challenge level
- Keep a balance of goals that present varying levels of challenge

## Quick Tips for Creating Detailed and Realistic Action Plans

- Develop written action plans
- Establish target completion dates
- Determine what you need to do on a daily, weekly, and monthly basis to reach your goals
- Celebrate your progress
- Consider the obstacles you may face and develop a plan to overcome them
- Remain flexible
- Review and revise your action plans regularly

## Quick Tips for Identifying Compelling Inspirations

- Identify your true inspiration
- You can find inspiration anywhere
- Make sure your inspiration is compelling
- Connect with your inspiration daily
- Share your inspiration with others

## Quick Tips for Building Strong Networks of Support

- Challenging goals require help
- Determine what help you will need and who can best provide it
- Determine how you will get feedback on your progress
- Ask for the assistance you need
- Share your plans with your supporters
- Be willing to help others

# Step 1 GAIN Plan Form

**GOAL:** Set a specific and challenging goal.    Date: _____

- Write your specific and challenging goal statement below. Begin with "I will . . ."

_____

_____

_____

- How will my success look and feel?

_____

_____

_____

- How will I measure my progress towards this goal?

_____

_____

_____

- How will this goal stretch me beyond my current abilities?

_____

_____

_____

Time + Energy + Skill + Expense = Challenge Level

***Rank the challenge level of this goal:*** Circle One Number

**5** = Most challenging    **4** = Very challenging    **3** = Challenging

**2** = Somewhat challenging    **1** = Not very challenging

*Form Individual-2*

# Step 2 G*A*IN Plan Form

**A**CTION PLAN: Create a detailed and realistic action plan.

Target Completion Date: _____

| Task | Date/On-Going |
|------|---------------|
| 1. _____ | |
| 2. _____ | |
| 3. _____ | |
| 4. _____ | |
| 5. _____ | |
| 6. _____ | |
| 7. _____ | |
| 8. _____ | |

**Obstacles that may inhibit me . . .**

_____

_____

**I will overcome these obstacles by . . .**

_____

_____

❏ **Target completion date and tasks written in calendar.**
As you make progress towards your goal, shade in the approximate percentage completed.

| | | | | |
|---|---|---|---|---|
| 0 | 25 | 50 | 75 | 100 |

# Step 3 GA*I*N Plan Form

*I*NSPIRATION: Identify your compelling Inspiration.

**My true inspiration for reaching this goal is:**

_____

_____

_____

_____

**Then ask yourself:**

- Have I identified my true inspiration for working towards this goal?
- Can I clearly picture my inspiration for reaching this goal?
  I see . . . _____

_____

_____

_____

**What will be my tangible connection to my inspiration?**

_____

_____

**How motivated am I by the inspiration I have identified?**
Circle One Number

**5** = Extremely motivated    **4** = Very motivated    **3** = Motivated
**2** = Somewhat motivated    **1** = Not very motivated

If your answer is less than 3, reconsider setting this goal.
If your answer is 3 or higher, go for it!

*Form Individual-4*

# Step 4 GAI*N* Plan Form

*N*ETWORK OF SUPPORT: Build a strong network of support.

**List a minimum of two people who will comprise my network of support. Indicate how they will help me.**

*Ensure that these people have the necessary knowledge and skills and are willing to help me!*

**Name:**          **How they will help me:**

1. _____

   _____

2. _____

   _____

3. _____

   _____

4. _____

   _____

**With at least one member of my network of support I have:**

❏ Reviewed the specificity and challenge of my goal.

❏ Reviewed my action plan and shared my potential obstacles and strategies for overcoming them.

❏ Shared my true inspiration for working towards this goal.

# My GAIN Plan

**G**oal

_____

_____

_____

**A**ction Plan (Summary Statement)

_____

_____

_____

**I**nspiration

_____

_____

_____

**N**etwork of Support

1. _____

2. _____

3. _____

4. _____

❑   My completed Action Plan is attached.

❑   I have shared my GAIN Plan with my network of support.

# Step 2 G*A*IN Plan Long Form

**A**CTION PLAN: Create a detailed and realistic action plan.

Target Completion Date: _____

| Task | Date/On-Going |
|---|---|
| 1. _____ | _____ |
| 2. _____ | _____ |
| 3. _____ | _____ |
| 4. _____ | _____ |
| 5. _____ | _____ |
| 6. _____ | _____ |
| 7. _____ | _____ |
| 8. _____ | _____ |
| 9. _____ | _____ |
| 10. _____ | _____ |
| 11. _____ | _____ |
| 12. _____ | _____ |
| 13. _____ | _____ |
| 14. _____ | _____ |
| 15. _____ | _____ |

# Step 2 G**A**IN Plan Long Form

**A**CTION PLAN: Create a detailed and realistic action plan.

**Obstacles that may inhibit me . . .**

_____

_____

_____

_____

_____

**I will overcome these obstacles by . . .**

_____

_____

_____

_____

_____

❑ **Target completion date and tasks written in calendar.**
As you make progress towards your goal, shade in the approximate percentage completed.

| | | | |
|---|---|---|---|
| 0 | 25 | 50 | 75 | 100 |

# Team GAIN Planning Tools

*Individual commitment to a group effort—that is what makes a team work, a company work, a society work, a civilization work.*

Vincent Lombardi

Think back to a time when you were part of a really successful team, a team that consistently reached its goals. A team you were proud to be on. Make sure you have a specific team in mind. Think about the people on the team; picture their faces. It doesn't matter what type of team comes to mind, as long as it was successful. Maybe it was a sports team, a work team, or a group of volunteers working for a common cause. Now remember some of the team's challenging goals. **Don't continue reading until you have a specific, successful team experience in mind.**

*Can you remember how it felt to work together with your teammates towards a common goal? Can you remember the sense of satisfaction you had when you succeeded and celebrated as a team?*

You can probably recall this experience in great detail. Working on a successful team, towards a worthwhile goal, is extremely rewarding.

Now think back to a time when you were on a team that was not so successful. Maybe you met your goal, but it was a struggle all along the way. When you did finish, there was no celebration, only a collective sigh of relief that the experience was over.

What made these two experiences so different? Why was it so great to be on one team and such a drag to be on the other?

Obviously, there is no single answer to this question, but oftentimes teams that struggle have not identified one or more components required to create a successful Team GAIN Plan. They have not set specific and challenging team goals, created detailed and realistic team action plans, identified compelling team inspirations, or built strong team networks of support.

This section will help you set and achieve your team goals. It will provide you with the information, tools, and resources you need to develop winning Team GAIN Plans. It will also help you to better facilitate team discussions about goals, roles, and responsibilities. You will find a list of critical questions that every team should consider each time they set a new, challenging team goal.

# Team GAIN Planning

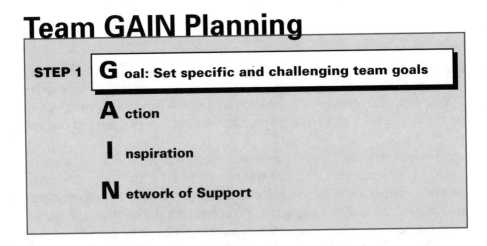

| STEP 1 | **G** oal: Set specific and challenging team goals |

**A** ction

**I** nspiration

**N** etwork of Support

## Successful Teams Set Specific and Challenging Goals

Think back to the successful team experience you identified earlier. Were the team's goals clear to everyone? Were team members able to anticipate how success would look and feel? Did the goals provide the team with an appropriate level of challenge? Most likely you answered "Yes" to all of these questions.

Teams need goals that give them clear targets. Team members need to be able to visualize how success will look and feel. Big projects must be broken down into smaller parts, giving team members a better ability to measure their progress. All of this requires specific goals. Teams with specific goals can focus their collective energy with much greater precision, allowing them to reach their goals faster and more efficiently.

To perform exceptionally, teams also need goals that provide the right level of challenge. With too little challenge, team members lose interest. Also, they don't feel any true sense of accomplishment when the goals are reached. On the other hand, when a team's goals are too challenging, members end up frustrated and disappointed. The right level of challenge, though, can motivate a team better than anything else. It forces members to rally together and creates a sense of energy and excitement for everyone involved.

Just like individuals, it's wise for teams, when possible, to balance the level of challenge of the goals they are working on. The right balance of challenge among the team's goals encourages every team member to dig deep and perform up to his or her highest potential. When this happens, the team becomes unstoppable. *The first step in developing winning Team GAIN Plans is to set specific and challenging team goals.*

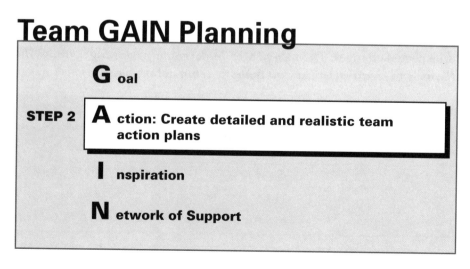

# Team GAIN Planning

**G** oal

STEP 2    **A** ction: Create detailed and realistic team action plans

**I** nspiration

**N** etwork of Support

## Successful Teams Create Detailed and Realistic Action Plans

Thinking again back to your successful team experience, did your team have plans for reaching its goals? Did these plans provide enough detail that everyone knew what they had to do? Were the timelines realistic? Most likely you answered "Yes" to all of these questions.

A team without a plan is like an orchestra without sheet music. You may have the best musicians in the world, but it's going to be tough to get everyone playing the same tune.

Team success requires planning. It's rare to see a successful team without detailed and realistic action plans, whether it's the playbook for a sports team, a work team's strategic plans, or a volunteer team's charter. Successful teams always have a plan.

To be effective, a team's action plans need to provide enough detail so that everyone on the team understands their role. People need to know what tasks they are responsible for, and by when those tasks need to be completed. Each task should be written down and agreed upon at the outset. If the scope of the project changes, new actions will need to be added and assigned to specific team members. All of this planning requires team members to communicate regularly. *The Team GAIN Planning Discussion Questions* you will find later in this section ensure that everyone on the team understands the plan and their role in it.

Successful teams are good at anticipating the obstacles they may encounter. They discuss these potential obstacles and create contingency plans for overcoming them. Preparing for the difficulties they may face builds the team's confidence and gives them the flexibility to adapt to any unexpected changes. *The second step in developing winning Team GAIN Plans is to create detailed and realistic team action plans.*

# Team GAIN Planning

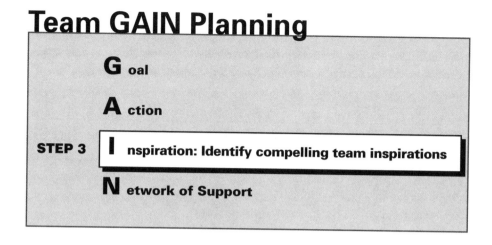

## Successful Teams Identify Compelling Individual and Team Inspirations

Again, thinking back to your successful team experience, was everyone on your team clear about why they were working towards the team's goals? Did team members have either an individual or collective inspiration to sustain them? Most likely this was the case.

Inspiration is a very personal thing. What inspires and motivates one person may not have the same effect on another. This makes it critical that team members discuss their individual and collective inspirations for succeeding. They need to ask themselves and each other, "Why are we working towards this goal? What will reaching this goal do for us, individually and collectively?" And, "Is our inspiration compelling enough to sustain us as we work towards this challenging goal?"

Not discussing these questions is risky. You have no way of knowing if the team is fully committed to reaching its goals. While everyone on the team does not need to be 100% motivated by every team goal, you do need a critical mass of people who are committed to success. These people will keep the team energized and will ensure that progress is being made. Helping a team reconnect with their inspiration is a powerful way to reinvigorate them when their motivation lulls.

Knowing what inspires your teammates is important. It gives you the power to help them stay committed through the challenges the team will inevitably face. *The third step in developing winning Team GAIN Plans is to identify your team's compelling inspirations for reaching the team's goals.*

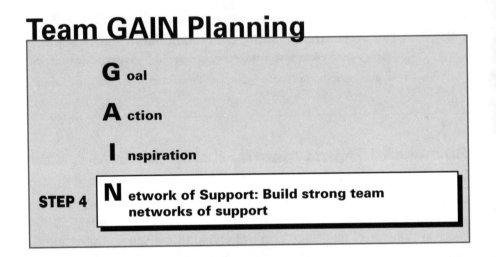

## Team GAIN Planning

**G** oal

**A** ction

**I** nspiration

STEP 4  **N** etwork of Support: Build strong team networks of support

## Successful Teams Build Strong Team Networks of Support

Think back one last time to your successful team experience. Did your team have the right players? Were team members willing and able to support one another? Did you have access to the people outside of the team that you needed to be successful? Chances are, if you succeeded, the answer to all of these questions is "Yes."

In order for teams to reach their challenging goals, they must provide one another with help and support. This support can take many forms, from providing information to listening, giving feedback, showing respect, mentoring, and much more.

When you are on a team, your teammates need to serve as the core members of your network of support. They are the people who can best understand the challenges you are facing and they are the most likely to be able to give you the assistance you need. If communication problems, conflicts, lack of respect, or other similar issues exist, they will derail your team. If these types of problems are hindering your team, seek help from outside the team—and do it soon.

Even on well-functioning teams, there are sometimes resources and people outside the team that are needed to be successful. Once these resources and individuals are identified, team members must work to gain access to them. Just like successful individuals, successful teams ask for the help they need. *The fourth step in developing winning Team GAIN Plans is to build strong team networks of support.*

## Team GAIN Planning Tools

By using the tools you will find in the rest of this section you can significantly increase any team's likelihood of succeeding. When a team you are a part of sets out towards a new goal, begin by conducting a Team GAIN Planning session. Start the session by answering the *Team GAIN Planning Discussion Questions* together. It's important that your team spend time answering these questions. Your answers will form the backbone of your Team GAIN Plan.

All of the tools you will find in the remainder of this section, along with additional team development resources, can be found on *Inspiration to Perspiration* online at *www.goalsuccess.com.*

## Quick Tips

### for Team GAIN Planning

- Teams need clear goals

- Teams need goals that present an appropriate level of challenge

- Team success requires planning

- Team action plans need to be detailed enough that each member is clear about their role

- Successful teams are good at anticipating obstacles and developing plans to overcome them

- Knowing what inspires your teammates will help you to motivate them

- Team members must provide each other with help and support in order for the team to reach its challenging goals

- Effective teams identify and seek help to resolve problems with communication, conflict, respect, and other interpersonal issues

- Review and revise your Team GAIN Plans regularly

# Team GAIN Planning Instructions

## *Team GAIN Planning Discussion*

Each time a team you're on wants to create a Team GAIN Plan for a challenging goal, begin by answering the *Team GAIN Planning Discussion Questions* together. Depending on the size of your team, you will want to set aside thirty to sixty minutes for this discussion. It is a good idea to record the team's answers to some of the discussion questions (especially those related to the action plan). You may want to have a designated note taker. The conversation that the *Team GAIN Planning Discussion Questions* generate will likely equate to 90% of the value of this process.

# Team GAIN Planning Forms

Your Team GAIN Planning discussion will generate the majority of the information you will need to complete the Team GAIN Planning forms. The entire team, or just a subgroup, can complete the Team GAIN Planning forms after the discussion. Set aside twenty to forty minutes to complete these forms. For teams with more than seven members I suggest using a subgroup. The forms will guide you step-by-step through the process of writing a Team GAIN Plan. When the forms are complete the team should reassemble to review the plan. Any concerns or suggested changes can be discussed at that time.

# Team GAIN Planning Discussion Questions

## GOAL: Specific and Challenging

1. What is our team's specific goal?
2. How will our success with this goal look and feel?
3. How will we measure our progress towards this goal?
4. How will this goal stretch us beyond our current abilities?

## ACTION PLAN: Detailed and Realistic

5. By when do we plan to accomplish this goal?
6. What are the specific tasks we will need to complete to reach this goal?
7. Who will be responsible for completing each of these tasks?
8. By when does each of these tasks need to be accomplished?
9. What obstacles may inhibit our team from reaching this goal?
10. How will we overcome these obstacles?

## INSPIRATION: Compelling

11. Why have we set this goal?
12. Have we identified our true inspiration for working towards this goal? *(Note: Team members may have different inspirations for reaching this goal. Encourage each person to articulate why they want the team to successfully accomplish this goal.)*
13. Can we clearly picture our inspirations for reaching this goal?
14. Are these inspirations compelling enough to carry us through to success?

## NETWORK OF SUPPORT: Strong

15. How will we support each other in reaching our goal?
16. What help do we need from people outside our team to reach this goal?
17. Who can provide us with this help?
18. Are these people willing to help our team?

# Step 1 Team GAIN Plan Form

**G**OAL: Set a specific and challenging team goal.   Date: _____

- Write your team's specific and challenging goal statement below. Begin with "We will . . . "

_____

_____

_____

- How will our success look and feel?

_____

_____

_____

- How will we measure our progress towards this goal?

_____

_____

_____

- How will this goal stretch us beyond our current abilities?

_____

_____

_____

Time + Energy + Skill + Expense = Challenge Level

***Rank the challenge level of this team goal:*** Circle One Number

**5** = Most challenging    **4** = Very challenging    **3** = Challenging

**2** = Somewhat challenging    **1** = Not very challenging

Transfer the Goal statement to your Team GAIN Plan Summary.

*Form Team-3*

# Step 2 Team G*A*IN Plan Form

**A**CTION PLAN: Create a detailed and realistic team action plan.

Target Completion Date: _____

Listed are all of the tasks required to reach our goal and who will be responsible for each of them.

| Task | Who's Responsible/By When |
|------|---------------------------|

1. _____

2. _____

3. _____

4. _____

5. _____

6. _____

7. _____

8. _____

**Listed are any obstacles that may inhibit our team from reaching this goal . . .**

_____

_____

**How will our team overcome these obstacles?** _____

_____

_____

*Individual team members may need to create their own action plans for accomplishing their specific tasks.

Attach this Action Plan to your Team GAIN Plan Summary.

# Step 3 Team GA*I*N Plan Form

*I*NSPIRATION: Identify your compelling Inspiration.

## Our inspiration for reaching this goal is:

_____

_____

_____

_____

*Individuals may identify their own personal inspiration for reaching the team's goal.

• Have we identified our true inspiration for working towards this goal?

• Can we clearly picture our inspiration for reaching this goal?

We see . . . _____

_____

_____

_____

**How motivated are we as a team by the inspiration we have identified?**
Circle One Number

**5** = Extremely motivated    **4** = Very motivated    **3** = Motivated
**2** = Somewhat motivated    **1** = Not very motivated

If your answer is less than 3, continue exploring what would motivate your Team.
If your answer is 3 or higher, go for it!

Transfer the inspiration statement to your Team GAIN Plan Summary.

*Form Team-5*

# Step 4 Team GAI*N* Plan Form

**N**ETWORK OF SUPPORT: Build a strong network of support.

**How will we support each other in reaching our goal?**

_____

_____

**List a minimum of two people (external to your team) who will be included in your network of support. Indicate how they will help you.**

*Ensure that these people have the necessary knowledge and skills and that they are willing to help!*

| Name: | How they will help us: |
|---|---|
| 1. _____ | _____ |
| | _____ |
| 2. _____ | _____ |
| | _____ |
| 3. _____ | _____ |
| | _____ |
| 4. _____ | _____ |
| | _____ |

Transfer the names of the people in your team's external network of support to your Team GAIN Plan Summary.

# Team GAIN Plan Summary

## Goal

We will: _____

_____

_____

## Action Plan (Summary Statement)

_____

_____

_____

## Inspiration (Collective)

_____

_____

_____

## Network of Support (Outside our team)

1. _____

2. _____

3. _____

4. _____

❑ Completed Team Action Plan attached.

❑ Team member's Individual Action Plans completed.

# Goal Setting Tools for Teens

*The greatest use of a life is to spend it for something that will outlast it.*

William James

Being a teenager today is exciting. You have an almost unlimited number of possibilities. You can truly have, be, or do almost anything you desire. Sometimes all these choices can be overwhelming. This section will help you continue the process of determining what you really want out of life.

*Goal Setting Tools for Teens* is written specifically for you, today's teenager. It's designed to help you get a handle on what goals you may want to set for your future. If you are not a teenager, don't stop reading yet! There are two possible reasons you may want to continue. First, if you have ever caught yourself wondering what you want to do when you grow up (whether you are 20, 30, 40, 50, or older) this section may help you figure it out. Second, if you are not a teenager you probably know one. Consider setting a goal to help a teenager you know begin to make some exciting decisions about his or her future. This section will give you the resources you need to help them.

For teens, this section will provide you with information and tools you can use to continue the life-long process of reaching your goals. Your goals may be educational, career, athletic, family, personal, or health-related. It doesn't matter. The resources you'll find here will help you clarify and begin to make plans to reach them.

As a teenager, everything you have read in the other sections of this book also applies to you. It is never too early to start setting goals. *Goal Setting Tools for Teens* will help you to get to the point where you can begin creating GAIN Plans for reaching your goals.

In Part One I suggested you dream big dreams, wish big wishes, and hold the highest of hopes. This is doubly true for you as a teen. You're living in a time when success is closer at hand for you than for anyone else in history. Don't limit your own potential. Go after your biggest dreams.

The first step in the GAIN Planning process is to set specific and challenging goals, but before you can do that, you need to be crystal clear about what you want. For many teens this is the most difficult part. All of your choices and potential paths can feel overwhelming, even frightening. Don't let these feelings paralyze you. One of the benefits of youth is that you can always change your mind.

The following section, *What I Really Want Out of Life!*, asks you to consider 50 questions. These questions are designed to help you clarify what is really important to you. The questions are broken into four categories: General, Educational, Career, and Personal. You may find that some of your answers to the different questions are similar. That's okay. The patterns that emerge will give you some clues about what goals you may want to set.

Consider the time you take answering these questions as an investment in a bank account called "Your Future." You'll get back the hour or two you take to do this exercise twenty times over. I promise.

# *What I Really Want Out of Life!* Instructions

*Make sure you have set aside at least one hour of uninterrupted time before you begin this exercise. It may take longer, but an hour will give you a solid start. Find a quiet comfortable place where you can be alone to think.*

Take out a few sheets of lined paper. At the top of the first sheet write, *What I Really Want Out of Life!* The 50 questions beginning on this page are intended to make you think. But don't think too much about any individual question. Usually the first thing that pops into your head is the most honest. You may not be able to answer some of the questions right away. That's fine. Go back to them when you're finished. Some questions may seem unimportant. Try to answer them anyway. They may become important later. Make sure you write out each question and then write out your answer. If you prefer, you can complete this exercise online at *www.goalsuccess.com.*

## *General*

1. What makes me happy?
2. What do I enjoy doing?
3. What am I really good at?
4. What would I like to try?
5. What do I value most?
6. What do I daydream about achieving?
7. Whom do I admire? Why?
8. What social problems bother me the most?
9. If I could solve one of these social ills, which one would I choose?
10. Whom would I most like to help?
11. What inspires me?
12. What motivates me?
13. What am I passionate about?
14. What volunteer activities do I currently enjoy?
15. What volunteer activities do I think I would enjoy?

## *Educational*

16. How important is education to me? Why?
17. What subjects do I enjoy?
18. In what subjects do I excel?
19. What subjects do I find difficult?
20. What would I like to learn (list 10 things)?
21. What languages would I like to learn?
22. What is the highest level of education I hope to achieve (high school graduate, associates degree, bachelors, masters, M.D., Ph.D., D.D.S.)?

## *Career*

23. What types of careers interest me?
24. If I could do anything at all for a living what would it be?
25. What are my top five dream jobs?
26. Which one do I think I'd enjoy the most?
27. Which one do I think I'd be the best at?
28. How important is money to me? Why?

## *Personal*

29. Where in the world would I like to visit?
30. Where would I like to live?
31. What, if any, athletic goals do I have?
32. What, if anything, would I like to improve about my health or fitness level?
33. What health concerns do I have for the future?
34. What health risks run in my family (heart disease, cancer, etc.)?
35. What are my most important relationships?
36. What are my three best personality traits?
37. What three personality traits would I most like to improve?
38. Where do I picture myself in two years?
39. What have I done that makes me the most proud?
40. What scares me the most?
41. Do I plan to get married?
42. Do I want children?

### Complete the Following Sentences

43. "To me success is . . ."
44. "To me happiness is . . ."
45. "My greatest strength is . . ."
46. "I feel most fulfilled when . . ."
47. "I will know I am successful when . . ."
48. "I am happiest when . . . "
49. "In five years I see myself . . . "
50. "In 10 years I see myself . . . "

# Goals

Congratulations! You've completed the hardest part. Your answers to the "What I Really Want Out of Life!" questions will guide many of your future decisions. They will also provide you with the raw material you need to begin setting goals today.

The next step is to review your answers. As you do, look for clues about what goals you want to further explore. As you read back over your answers, what patterns do you notice? What connections do you see?

When you review your answers, highlight (with a hi-lighter) any that relate to a goal you might want to set. For example, if under education you indicated that you want to graduate from college and that is really important to you, highlight it.

When you are done highlighting your answers, some potential goals should become clear. Choose up to 16 and write them in the Goals to Further Explore Form. Make sure some are long-term goals and others short-term. Some may be big enough that you will end up breaking them into smaller parts. You are not yet committing to doing any of these things. You are only committing to further exploring them as possibilities.

# Action Plans

Hopefully, you have identified a few goals you are interested in further exploring. Now you need to gather information to help you decide which goals to pursue. This will require that you do some detective work. Your

*Form Teen-2*

# Goals to Further Explore Form

## General

1. _____

2. _____

3. _____

4. _____

## Educational

5. _____

6. _____

7. _____

8. _____

## Career

9. _____

10. _____

11. _____

12. _____

## Personal

13. _____

14. _____

15. _____

16. _____

job is to learn as much as you can about what it would take to reach the goals you are considering. Here is just some of what you'll want to know:

- What would be a realistic timeline for this goal?
- What tasks would be required to reach this goal?
- What obstacles might I encounter?
- How could I overcome these obstacles?
- Whose help would I need?
- What, if anything, will it cost?
- What will I have to give up to reach this goal?

How can you find the answers to these questions? There are lots of ways: surf the Internet, go to the library, buy books at the bookstore, take classes, read newspaper and magazine articles, and talk to as many people as you can.

One of the best ways to learn what you need to know is to find people who have accomplished the goals you are considering. Talk to them and ask them tons of questions. If you are considering medicine as a profession, talk with as many doctors as possible. If you think you want to move to New York, talk to some New Yorkers. What if you think you might want to be a governor? You don't have to call the governor's mansion. Talk to people in local politics (city council people, school board members, etc.). They can give you some insight into politics as a profession. You will find that most people are willing to share their experiences with you. A benefit to this approach is that when you do decide which goals to pursue, you will already have identified people for your networks of support.

It doesn't matter where you get the information you need. The important thing is that you get it. Learn as much as possible before you commit yourself to any major goals.

# Inspirations

You will also want to determine if the goals you are considering will fulfill you. To know this you need to be clear about what inspires you. Your answers to some of the *What I Really Want Out of Life!* questions are a good place to start. Look carefully at how you answered questions like, "What makes me happy? What am I passionate about? Who would I most like to help?" and "What have I done that makes me the most proud?" Your answers to these questions tell you what's important to you and what's not. Make sure that the goals you set are congruent with what you discover.

# Networks of Support

Even before you decide exactly which goals you will work towards, you can begin identifying potential people for your networks of support. These people can serve as important resources as you make decisions about your future. Make sure you enlist people who are invested in your success.

As you identify potential people for your networks of support, consider these questions:

- Whose opinions do I most respect?
- Whom do I know who has achieved the things I am considering?
- Whom do I know who may have connections that could help me?

Some of the people you may want to consider for your networks of support include:

- Parents
- Family members: aunts, uncles, grandparents, cousins, older siblings
- Friends of your parents
- Friends of your older siblings
- Teachers
- School administrators
- Coaches
- Neighbors

Make a list of 16 people you respect and would consider asking for help. Identify different people for different goals, when appropriate. Try to identify at least three people who you think might be more challenging to contact. For example, if you are a figure skater and are considering going out for the Olympic team, you might identify an Olympic skater you admire. Once you do, you can do your best to get into contact with him or her. Use the My Potential Networks of Support Form to capture your list.

# My Potential Networks of Support Form

Goal                                   Potential Supporter

1. _____
.

2. _____

3. _____

4. _____

5. _____

6. _____

7. _____

8. _____

9. _____

10. _____

11. _____

12. _____

## Challenging People to Contact

13. _____

14. _____

15. _____

16. _____

Once you have identified some preliminary people for your networks of support, choose two you respect. Share your Goals to Further Explore Form with them and as many of your fifty *What I Really Want out of Life!* answers as you are willing. Ask them for help in making decisions about which goals are right for you.

This is an awesome time in your life. You have almost endless opportunities in front of you. All you need to do is figure out which paths you want to take. If you have completed the exercises in this section you should have a clearer picture of where you want to go. When you are ready, you can go to the individual and/or Team GAIN Planning sections and use the forms there to set whatever goals you have chosen.

# Quick Tips

## for Teen Goal Setting

- Don't limit your potential; go for your big dreams
- Remember that you can always change your mind
- Set a mixture of long-term and short-term goals
- Learn as much as you can before you commit yourself to any major goals
- Talk to people you respect who've achieved the goals you are considering
- Make sure the goals you set are congruent with what's important to you
- Develop strong networks of support for all your goals

At *www.goalsuccess.com* you will find more information and resources on selecting and setting goals. Also, please e-mail me at *djacobson@goalsuccess.com* with any questions. I promise I will reply to you personally. See, you already have one new person in your network of support.

Good luck. Enjoy the process of making your dreams reality!

# The Finish Line

*The man who can drive himself further once the effort gets painful is the man who will win.*

Sir Roger Bannister

Throughout this book it has been my goal to provide you with the information, inspiration, and tools you need to achieve your goals. As we come to the end of our journey together, I must admit that I have given you only 90% percent of what you'll need to succeed. What is the last 10% percent, you ask? It's almost impossible to quantify. It's what we commonly refer to as passion, desire, drive, commitment, determination, belief, faith, or just sheer will. It is the willingness to push through whatever challenges confront you as you work towards your dreams. It's what separates good enough from truly exceptional. And it is inside each and every one of us if we are willing to access it.

While it's difficult to quantify this final 10% required for success, we know it when we see it. And we can see examples of it all around us. We see it in the weary eyes of a medical student who has sacrificed sleep and personal time for years on end to achieve his dream of becoming a doctor. We see it in the steely gaze of a marathoner as she steadily puts one foot in front of the other until she reaches the finish line. And hopefully you've seen flashes of it in yourself; those times when you knew, with every fiber of your being, that you were going to succeed.

## The Miracle Mile

*A great example of the importance of believing in yourself is the story of Sir Roger Bannister and his "Miracle Mile."*

In 1954, Roger Bannister did what many considered to be impossible. He ran a mile in under four minutes. Until Bannister's record-breaking run, the four-minute "barrier" had been considered by many to be beyond the physical limits of the human body. This commonly held belief did not deter Bannister. In fact, it was a key motivating factor for him. Bannister trained hard and gained as much knowledge as he could about the mechanical aspects of running. But, ultimately, it was his belief that it was possible that kept him committed in the face of so many doubters.

Roger Bannister was named *Sports Illustrated's* first Sportsman of the Year in 1954 for his accomplishment of running a mile in three minutes and 59.4 seconds. Yet, astonishingly, Bannister's record stood for only 46 days. Within a year of Bannister's record, 37 more runners had run a mile in under four minutes. And two years later 300 runners had broken the four minute "barrier." By 2001, the world record for the mile was down to 3:43.13. It turned out that the four-minute mile "barrier" was not physical at all but psychological. Beyond having the physical aptitude, Bannister had the psychological attitude that it could be done. When Bannister was asked by *Sports Illustrated* to explain his success he said simply, "It is the ability to take more out of yourself than you've got." Roger Bannister's belief that he could succeed made all the difference.

## You Are What You Think

Your attitudes and beliefs will make all the difference for you as well. Don't be deterred by the doubts or discouragement of others. You are the architect of your dreams and your life, and only you can decide what's possible. In many ways you are what you think. When you think small, you act small, which creates small results. But when you think big, you act big, which brings huge results. So for goodness sake, think big. In fact, think bigger than you have ever thought before. If anything is going to stop you from making your dreams reality, don't let it to be your own self-limiting beliefs. When thinking about how you want your life to be in the future, pull out all the stops and imagine it exactly how you would like it to be. The clearer you can picture what you want, the better. There is good evidence that clearly visualizing your goals on a regular basis is a contributing factor to success.

## The Hardest Thing about Committing— Is Committing

Once you know what you want and can clearly visualize it, you must commit to going out and getting it. For many people, this is the hardest part. We all know people who have talked about doing this or that, sometimes for years, but never commit to it and take action. In fact, most of us are probably guilty of this for one goal or another. And there are always good reasons to not commit. It isn't the right time, the risks are too great, we have other responsibilities, etc. While these reasons are probably all valid, the fact is there will never be a perfect time when the risk is small and we don't have other responsibilities. We must commit in spite of our good reasons not to. And once we do, we must have faith that we will succeed. This requires courage. The courage to take a risk. The courage to believe in ourselves. And the courage to move towards what we want in the face of all the challenges we encounter.

## The More You Risk, the More You Have to Gain

Moving towards our challenging goals requires us to take risks. We have to sail our ships outside the safety of the harbor, often into uncharted waters. When we do this it's helpful to remember that the more we risk, the more we have to gain. No one who is extremely successful at anything got that way by always playing it safe. This is true for you as well. You must be willing to take some risks to get the big gains you're looking for in your life. I'm not suggesting you throw caution to the wind and take reckless chances. But taking the right calculated risks, at the right time, can make all the difference. Rely on people you trust, the people in your networks of support, to help you determine when the risk and the timing is right for you.

## Celebrate Your Failures and Your Successes

While the more you risk the more you have to gain, it wouldn't be a risk if there wasn't the chance of failing. The fact is, if you never fail you're probably not working towards challenging enough goals. If you have failed, I mean really failed, not just never started trying, then congratulations. It means you're taking chances and are working towards your big dreams. You should celebrate the fact that you have the courage to attempt something so difficult.

Another way to look at failure is as a learning experience. At minimum you learned what NOT to do to reach your goal. There are often many valuable lessons that come with failing. When I talk with successful managers and executives about their most important learning experiences, they often involve situations that, from the outside, look like failures. The difference is that these successful people took the lessons from what went wrong and used them to become even more successful in the future.

While it might be hard to celebrate your failures, it should be easy to celebrate your successes. Even so, often we don't take the time to really stop and celebrate what we've accomplished. This is especially true for those of us who are very ambitious. Our reaction to reaching a goal is often to immediately set another one. That's all right, but you've got to celebrate what you have attained.

Just as your failures hold important lessons, so do your successes. When you take time to celebrate those successes, think about what you have learned that you can apply to future goals. You did something right, so make sure you add those tools to your tool belt.

**Success is not final, failure not fatal: it is the courage to continue that counts.**

*Sir Winston Churchill*

## Never, Ever Give Up

The reality of striving for challenging goals is that you will meet with both failure and success. The key to persevering and emerging victorious is to NEVER, EVER GIVE UP. No matter what happens, no matter how challenging it gets, or how many set-backs you encounter, keep moving forward. The stories in Part Two are the best evidence I can give you of the power we have to overcome seemingly insurmountable odds. You heard from people who have endured enough pain and challenge for a lifetime. People who made the choice not to recede in the face of their struggles but to fight harder to get what they wanted. They did it, and you can too.

## Quick Tips

### for Success

- You are what you think—so think big
- The hardest thing about committing— is committing
- The more you risk, the more you have to gain
- Celebrate your failures and your successes
- Never, ever give up

## No Return Receipt Requested

At the outset of this book I shared with you how a single discarded post-card changed the course of my life. It has led me to pursue and reach goals I'd never before considered. I believe these types of opportunities present themselves to us all, at various times in our lives. The problem is that these "postcards" are never delivered return receipt requested. So it can be easy to discard them, as I almost did. To avoid missing these opportunities, you must remain open to all the possibilities around you. And, when you recognize a potential opportunity, explore it with an open mind and a willingness to imagine the possibilities. If it seems right go for it!

## Establish Five Mile-Markers for Your Success

How do you end a book about reaching your goals? You set some goals of course. To ensure that you put what you have learned into action, I encourage you to establish some mile-markers to help you measure your progress. What will you do today, this week, this month, this year, and this lifetime to make your dreams reality? Write some commitments to yourself on the following page and then put the book down and go out and start making them happen.

# Five Mile-Markers for My Success

**Mile–marker 1: Today**

_____

_____

_____

**Mile–marker 2: This Week**

_____

_____

_____

**Mile–marker 3: This Month**

_____

_____

_____

**Mile–marker 4: This Year**

_____

_____

_____

**Mile–marker 5: This Lifetime**

_____

_____

_____

# About the Author

D avid A. Jacobson is the founder and president of Goal Success, Inc., a company dedicated to maximizing the potential of individuals, teams, and organizations. Goal Success designs and delivers customized leadership development, team building, and executive coaching solutions to many Fortune 100 companies.

For over a decade David has been working with individuals and teams from around the world, helping them to reach their personal and professional goals. His approach is highly interactive and experiential. As a skilled speaker and facilitator who believes in an action learning philosophy, David is committed to making learning and development fun.

Goal Success' areas of specialization include: leadership development and team building programs, executive coaching, motivational speaking, team vision, values, and mission clarification, facilitating individual and team assessment and feedback processes, and adventure-based learning experiences.

David lives in San Diego with his wife Shari and his son Sean. They enjoy taking advantage of all the outdoor activities that San Diego has to offer.

Contact Goal Success for information about training, development, and consulting services or to have David Jacobson inspire your group at your next meeting or event!

Goal Success, Inc.
10601 Tierrasanta Blvd., Suite 402
San Diego, CA 92124
Phone: 800-GOAL-4-IT (800-462-5448)
Fax: 858-715-1616
E-mail: *djacobson@goalsuccess.com*
*www.goalsuccess.com*

# Contributors

All of the stories you read in this book were written from the hearts of the people who experienced them. You will find basic biographical information about each story contributor here. To learn more about their journeys, read updates on their lives, see their personal photo albums, or send them a message, visit *www.goalsuccess.com*.

**Pamela S. Beemer** is the director of benefits in the office of human resources at Michigan State University. She first became involved with Team In Training in July 1998 at the urging of a pediatric intensive care nurse who cared for her son during his courageous battle with leukemia. Pam has completed four marathons as a TNT participant. In addition to her lifetime commitment to raising funds, she also serves on the board of directors of the Michigan chapter of The Leukemia & Lymphoma Society.

**Alison Boudreau** works as community director with a non-profit organization in the San Francisco Bay Area. She first got involved with TNT in the winter of 1999. In 2000, she became a mentor for the summer run team. After completing the Dublin, Ireland, marathon she ventured into triathlons as a PR captain and mentor. Her story is dedicated to the loving memory of her inspirational Iron Teammate, Louie Bonpua, whose spirit continues to live on in the hearts of those he touched.

**Barry Bouse** is the supervisor of receiving for Best Access Systems in Indianapolis, IN. Barry first got involved with TNT in January 1997 and has since run five marathons and two half marathons. In 1998, Barry and his wife Betty created *Chad's Challenge Memorial Golf Tournament* with proceeds supporting the Leukemia & Lymphoma Society. In June of 2002 Barry became a member of the board of trustees for the Indiana chapter. Barry plans to expand his TNT experience to include a century bike race in 2003 and possibly a triathlon in 2004.

**Bruce Cleland** is the president and chief executive officer of Campbell & Company, an investment management firm located in Baltimore, MD. Bruce established Team In Training in 1988 as a volunteer effort inspired by his daughter Georgia's battle with leukemia. His inaugural team raised more than $320,000 for leukemia research. He still participates as a TNT athlete, most recently competing in the Athens-to-Atlanta in-line skating race. He is married with four children and lives in Ruxton, MD.

**Barry Costa** teaches carpet repair, reinstallation, and water damage restoration throughout the United States, Canada, the U.K., and Australia. Inspired by his daughter Kimberly, Barry joined TNT for the 2001 Walt Disney World Marathon. Barry and his family raised $16,000 in 2001 and over $21,000 in 2002! Barry is committed to honoring Kim's memory by continuing to run marathons until a cure is found.

**Lucy De Vries Duffy** lives on Cape Cod. When not running, she can be found kayaking or off-roading at Nauset Beach with her family, including four sons and six grandchildren, with a seventh on the way. Since her husband's death, Lucy has continued to raise money for leukemia research. Since her 1986 New York Marathon she has raised approximately $200,000. In 2002, the Boston Leukemia & Lymphoma Society chapter honored Lucy by naming an annual Lucy Against Leukemia Award. Lucy is presently training for her 14th marathon, the 2003 Boston Marathon. She will be celebrating her 70th birthday.

**Shawna Fisher** is a licensed social worker in the state of Utah and currently works as a youth counselor. Shawna was diagnosed with non-Hodgkin lymphoma in March of 1998. Not only was she an honored patient for TNT, she also completed her first marathon as a team member in 2001 while still undergoing cancer treatments. Just days before carrying the Olympic torch for the Salt Lake 2002 Winter Olympics, Shawna went into remission.

**Mike Fitzpatrick** is an assistant district manager for Williams Gas Pipeline-Transco in Grover, NC. Mike began training with the Charlotte chapter of TNT in July 2001 and has run the Walt Disney World Marathon and the Country Music Half Marathon and plans to continue competing in support of TNT. His hobbies include flying, camping, traveling, and coaching the Orioles—his son's T-Ball team.

**Tim Hamburger** is a senior institutional healthcare representative for Pfizer, Inc. in Pittsburgh, PA. He first got involved with TNT in January 1998 and ran the inaugural Rock 'n' Roll Marathon in San Diego. He continues to be inspired on a daily basis by his patient hero, Matt Lewis. Since 1998, Tim has helped raise nearly $48,000 for blood cancer research and patient aid. Tim currently serves on his local chapter's board of trustees and he helped create the cycling component of TNT for the Western Pennsylvania/West Virginia chapter in 1999, which has generated more than $500,000!

**Anthony Iacono** has completed six TNT marathons for his son Paul, who serves as the national patient youth ambassador for the Leukemia & Lymphoma Society. In January 1998, Anthony broke the Society's national record for donations raised by a single runner by raising more than $100,000! Anthony is the CEO and town administrator of Secaucus, NJ, and he has served as the maitre de at Giants Stadium. In spite of his busy schedule, Anthony still manages to log 30 miles per week.

**Shari Jacobson** is an elementary school teacher for San Diego City Schools. She is currently on a leave of absence from teaching to raise her son Sean and work for Goal Success, Inc. Her hobbies include travel, writing, and training for sprint triathlons. Shari first got involved with TNT in January 1998, when she ran the inaugural Rock 'n' Roll Marathon with her husband David. That was Shari's first marathon. Since then she has been working with her husband to complete *Inspiration to Perspiration*.

**Ashlee Moskwa** joined TNT as an honored patient in the spring of 2000, one year after being diagnosed with non-Hodgkin lymphoma. Ashlee cheered on competitors in the Walt Disney World Marathon in January 2001 and walked the half marathon with her mother the following year. For the past three years she has been an avid volunteer with the Leukemia & Lymphoma Society's Light The Night Walk. Since receiving rehabilitation for two strokes caused by her cancer treatment, Ashlee has continually worked to raise funds for cancer awareness and talks publicly about her experiences. She is currently a college freshman at Johns Hopkins University.

# More *Inspiration to Perspiration*

W e are currently collecting stories for a sequel to *Inspiration to Perspiration* and for *Inspiration to Perspiration* online. If you or someone you know has an inspiring true story of courage, hope, survival, perseverance, or reaching challenging goals, we want to hear from you. It can be about a Team In Training experience or something completely unrelated. The only criteria is that it is true and you believe it will inspire others to reach for their goals.

We are also looking for stories for some special editions of *Inspiration to Perspiration,* including stories about teenagers, athletes, women, parents, and business success among others.

Some helpful suggestions:

1. Tell your story in your own words, and write it in a way that will inspire and motivate others.

2. Stir the readers' emotions by putting them in the middle of the action.

3. Share any lessons you've learned and any positive results that have come from your experience.

Please submit stories online, via e-mail, by fax, or by mail. Include your contact information so we can get back to you. If you have any questions or need further information, please contact us.

You can submit your story online at *www.goalsuccess.com.*

GOAL SUCCESS, Inc.
10601 Tierrasanta Blvd., Suite 402
San Diego, CA 92124
Phone: 800-GOAL-4-IT (800-462-5448)
Fax: 858-715-1616
E-mail: *info@goalsuccess.com*

# The Leukemia &
# Lymphoma Society ®

## Fighting Blood-Related Cancers

The Leukemia & Lymphoma Society®, based in White Plains, NY, is the world's largest voluntary health organization dedicated to funding blood cancer research, education and patient services. The Society's mission is to cure leukemia, lymphoma, Hodgkin's disease and myeloma, and to improve the quality of life of patients and their families. Since its founding in 1949, the Society has provided more than $320 million for research specifically targeting blood cancers. For additional information, or to make a donation, please contact the Society at 800-955-4572 or visit *www.leukemia-lymphoma.org*

Team In Training, The Leukemia & Lymphoma Society's signature national fundraising initiative, is the world's largest endurance sports training program. It offers runners, walkers, and cyclists of all levels the opportunity to compete in half marathons, marathons, century rides, and triathlons. Participants fundraise to support the event and to help the Society achieve its mission.

For more information, please call 800-482-TEAM or visit the program's website at *www.teamintraining.org*

# Easy Order Form

**Fax orders:** 858-715-1616. Fax this form.
**Telephone orders:** Call 800-GOAL-4-IT (800-462-5448) toll free.
**E-mail orders:** *orders@goalsuccess.com*
**Online orders:** *www.goalsuccess.com*
**Postal orders:** GOAL SUCCESS, Orders, 10601 Tierrasanta Blvd., Suite 402, San Diego, CA 92124-2605

**Please send me** _____ copies of *Inspiration to Perspiration.*

I understand that I may return any of them for a full refund for any reason.

Name _____

Address_____

City/State/Zip_____

Phone _____

Email _____

**Sales tax:** Please add 7.75% for books shipped to California addresses. Make checks payable to Goal Success, Inc.

## Shipping

U.S.: $4.00 for first book and $1.00 for each additional book.

My check or money order for $_____ is enclosed.

Please charge my:   ❑ Visa   ❑ MasterCard   ❑ Discover   ❑ AMEX

Card number:_____

Name on Card: _____ Exp. Date:_____

Signature: _____